New Directions for
Community Colleges

Arthur M. Cohen
EDITOR-IN-CHIEF

Florence B. Brawer
ASSOCIATE EDITOR

Carrie B. Kisker
Edward Francis Ryan
MANAGING EDITORS

D1524282

DATE DUE

Community College
Missions in the
21st Century

Barbara K. Townsend
Kevin J. Dougherty
EDITORS

Number 136 • Winter 2006
Jossey-Bass
San Francisco

COMMUNITY COLLEGE MISSIONS IN THE 21ST CENTURY
Barbara K. Townsend, Kevin J. Dougherty (eds.)
New Directions for Community Colleges, no. 136

Arthur M. Cohen, Editor-in-Chief
Florence B. Brawer, Associate Editor

NEW DIRECTIONS FOR COMMUNITY COLLEGES (ISSN 0194-3081, electronic ISSN 1536-0733) is part of The Jossey-Bass Higher and Adult Education Series and is published quarterly by Wiley Subscription Services, Inc., A Wiley Company, at Jossey-Bass, 989 Market Street, San Francisco, California 94103-1741. Periodicals Postage Paid at San Francisco, California, and at additional mailing offices. POSTMASTER: Send address changes to New Directions for Community Colleges, Jossey-Bass, 989 Market Street, San Francisco, California 94103-1741.

SUBSCRIPTIONS cost $80.00 for individuals and $195.00 for institutions, agencies, and libraries in the United States. Prices subject to change. See order form at the back of book.

EDITORIAL CORRESPONDENCE should be sent to the Editor-in-Chief, Arthur M. Cohen, at the Graduate School of Education and Information Studies, University of California, Box 951521, Los Angeles, California 90095-1521. All manuscripts receive anonymous reviews by external referees.

New Directions for Community Colleges is indexed in Current Index to Journals in Education (ERIC).

Microfilm copies of issues and articles are available in 16mm and 35mm, as well as microfiche in 105mm, through University Microfilms Inc., 300 North Zeeb Road, Ann Arbor, Michigan 48106-1346.

CONTENTS

EDITORS' NOTES

The community college's societal and functional missions have been contested throughout the institution's history. Community college societal missions are the "overarching institutional purposes" serving to "justify the institution to external constituencies" (Doucette, Richardson, and Fenske, 1985, p. 193). These missions involve sometimes contradictory ideas, such as democratizing higher education by providing open access for disadvantaged students and demonstrating institutional accountability for students' academic success, or ensuring social mobility through education and serving the needs of local communities, especially their businesses and industries. Functional missions, defined as the "specific activities in which institutions actually engage" to pursue a particular societal mission (Doucette, Richardson, and Fenske, 1985, p. 193), typically include transfer education, vocational or technical education, continuing education, developmental education, and community service. These functional missions, as well as the societal missions they embody, are under debate. For example, some say the societal mission of providing access to higher education through community colleges is best achieved by a rigorous academic transfer curriculum that will help students attain a baccalaureate. Others insist that students are best served through workforce development programs that target local and statewide businesses and offer graduates more immediate economic benefits.

Changing demographic, economic, and social pressures repeatedly splinter and reform individual community colleges' emphases on different institutional missions and their expression in college functions. And different college constituencies support different missions, depending on their idea of what higher education should be and what role community colleges should play in the educational system. What makes decisions about community college missions so intriguing is that every position taken has merit, depending on one's perspective on the role of community colleges in the higher education system and in society.

Given that implicit societal missions underlie functional missions such as enrollment management, honors programs, and continuing education, institutional leaders and policymakers need to be more conscious of the interplay between the two concepts of mission. They would also benefit from insight into the tensions between the two-year college's functional and societal missions, as well as the internal and external forces that affect them. This volume incorporates both perspectives on institutional missions.

NEW DIRECTIONS FOR COMMUNITY COLLEGES, no. 136, Winter 2006 © Wiley Periodicals, Inc.
Published online in Wiley InterScience (www.interscience.wiley.com) • DOI: 10.1002/cc.253

Along the way this volume also addresses the impact on community college missions of changing student demographics, such as the projected increase in high school graduates by 2012 and the rising, but ever more restricted, state budget allocations. The increasing proportion of minority, immigrant, and younger community college students has major implications for which functions community colleges wish to emphasize. At the same time, those wishes operate in an environment where state and local governments—although in better fiscal shape than they were a few years ago—are still reluctant to sharply increase their spending on higher education and greatly expand community college functions.

We begin the volume with an introductory chapter that sets the stage for subsequent discussions about specific societal and functional missions. In Chapter One, Kevin Dougherty and Barbara Townsend describe the various approaches to defining and classifying community college missions, examine how those missions have varied over time and across states and regions, analyze how and why missions may conflict, and speculate on the future of community college missions.

Following this introduction, the volume moves to commentary about two of the community college's primary societal missions. Chapter Two presents a case for what has long been the community college's dominant societal mission: open access for educational attainment. Its authors, Henry Shannon and Ronald Smith, assert that open access should continue to be the community college's dominant societal mission. The authors also note various threats to this mission and suggest ways to strengthen it in response to these challenges. In Chapter Three, George Higginbottom and Richard Romano argue that another one of the community college's societal missions is educating people for what the authors call "civic competence." They maintain that general education, although an important curricular function of transfer education, is also vital in preparing a democratic citizenry. After reviewing the goals of general education and describing a typical general-civic education program, the authors discuss various obstacles to implementing such a program, as well as opportunities for expanding general education for civic competence.

In Chapter Four, Barbara Townsend and Kristin Wilson discuss one of the original curricular missions of the two-year college. After reviewing studies about transfer rates and the performance of community college students after transfer, the authors focus on current developments influencing transfer rates and the transfer function in general and speculate about its future as a dominant curricular mission.

The development of community college honors programs can be seen as part of the functional transfer mission, but also as an extension of the societal mission of expanding access to higher education. In Chapter Five, Deborah Floyd and Alexandria Holloway describe the development and current status of honors programs in community colleges, highlighting in particular the Honors College at Miami Dade College in Florida. Although some argue that honors programs are elitist and therefore do not belong in a community college, these authors contend that the programs represent an important effort to meet student needs, including access to the kind of special programs found at many four-year institutions.

In Chapter Six, James Jacobs and Kevin Dougherty analyze the functional mission of workforce development, focusing on current and possible future trajectories for this mission. In particular, they discuss how workforce development is suffering from a sharp decline in corporate demand and state support, as well as the emergence of new competitors. The chapter then describes two likely, but potentially contradictory, paths that lie before community college workforce development: a focus on occupational programs that may eventually lead to a baccalaureate degree (the so-called new vocationalism) and a focus on providing skills and credentials to low-income adults.

Developmental education is a necessary, well-known, but not always well-regarded functional mission of the community college. In Chapter Seven, Carol Kozeracki and Bryan Brooks discuss factors affecting attitudes toward this community college mission and present a case study describing how Davidson County Community College (North Carolina) has reenvisioned its developmental education program so that faculty view this mission more positively.

Chapter Eight, by John Downey, Brian Pusser, and Kirsten Turner, examines another curricular function of community colleges—continuing education. Their chapter presents data from a national survey of continuing education programs in community colleges in order to describe continuing education offerings and the institutional purposes behind them. The authors then analyze future possibilities for continuing education, given dwindling state support and greater competition from for-profit institutions.

Curricular missions are not the only functional missions community colleges pursue. In Chapter Nine, Nancy Ritze examines the functional mission of enrollment management in the community college and how this function can affect a college's ability to carry out other functional and societal missions. Ritze analyzes how Bronx Community College (BCC) and other two-year institutions have implemented knowledge management and business intelligence tools and describes the important role institutional research plays in BCC's enrollment management efforts.

Finally, given the plethora of possible community college missions—both societal and functional—it behooves college leaders to prioritize missions in order to focus institutional resources on those deemed most vital to their institution's goals and values. Thus, the concluding chapter in this volume outlines a step-by-step process for setting mission priorities. In Chapter Ten, Christine and Irving McPhail provide a framework that allows college leaders to take the uniqueness of their institution into account when determining which missions to emphasize.

Collectively, these chapters aim to stimulate community college leaders to reexamine their institution's functional missions in the context of the community college's societal missions. Some chapters provide case studies illustrating how various functional missions such as enrollment management, honors programs, and developmental education can be addressed in specific institutional settings. Chapters providing a broader, more national perspective on such curricular functions as transfer education, workforce development, and continuing education are designed to stimulate institutional leaders, policymakers, and scholars of the community college to reflect more deeply about these functions and gauge their relative importance in the community college and in the greater system of higher education. Such reflection is also helpful in identifying—and mitigating—ways in which the unreflective pursuit of one mission may undercut the effectiveness of other missions. Finally, a framework for prioritizing missions at an institutional level is of benefit to all who must make decisions about whose needs must be met and with what resources—vital concerns for everyone in higher education today.

Barbara K. Townsend
Kevin J. Dougherty
Editors

Reference

Doucette, D. S., Richardson, R. C., and Fenske, R. H. "Defining Institutional Mission: Application of a Research Model." *Journal of Higher Education,* 1985, 56(2), 189–205.

BARBARA K. TOWNSEND *is professor of higher and continuing education at the University of Missouri-Columbia and a former community college faculty member and administrator.*

KEVIN J. DOUGHERTY *is associate professor of higher education and senior researcher at the Community College Research Center at Teachers College, Columbia University.*

1

*This chapter analyzes various ways of conceptualizing
the missions of the community college, describes how
those missions have varied over time and across geo-
graphical regions, and examines how missions comple-
ment and conflict with one another.*

Community College Missions: A Theoretical and Historical Perspective

Kevin J. Dougherty, Barbara K. Townsend

Questions and concerns about the community college's missions have recurred throughout the institution's history. Often these questions are framed in overly strong dualisms: Is the community college's mission to provide transfer education so that students can eventually attain a baccalaureate, or is it to offer workforce development to meet the needs of business and industry? Should two-year colleges focus on ensuring open access to higher education for all who desire it, or should they concentrate more on providing high-quality academic and occupational training?

Careful responses to these and other questions about appropriate institutional missions seem especially critical with the increasing visibility of community colleges. The institutions have attracted attention from several federal agencies, most state governments, and major foundations such as Ford and Lumina. A key source of this heightened interest is the increasing number of high school graduates who desire a college education, combined with limited spaces in four-year college freshman classes (partly due to reduced state funding of the public four-year sector). State-level funding cutbacks in higher education and the consequent rise in tuition at public institutions have led to soaring community college enrollments in many states, and many families see community colleges as the best financial bargain for the first two years of college.

Lots of competition!

With increased attention has come greater demand for community colleges to document their claims of success and allay continuing concerns over low transfer and degree attainment rates. Moreover, community college leaders and state policymakers face difficult decisions about which missions to emphasize, given limited resources, competing claims of various internal and external stakeholders, and tensions between various missions.

These decisions about mission are important, because they can shape community colleges in a number of ways. Missions orient community college officials as they react to changing conditions and decide whether and how to pursue new opportunities. Mission definitions also influence the rules and procedures community college and state officials use to make decisions about curriculum, student advising, and faculty hiring, and to assess the performance of community colleges (Bogart, 1994; Dougherty and Hong, 2006).

Given the importance of mission definitions, institutional leaders and governmental policymakers need to be more conscious of the multiple (and sometimes conflicting) missions of the community college, their evolution, and the tensions between them. In this chapter, we will examine how to determine what the missions of the community college are, what forces shape the development of missions, and what are the impacts of one or another set of missions on community colleges, their students, and their external environments. In doing this, we will address a key question: To the extent that community colleges can determine their missions, should they aim to be comprehensive, encompassing multiple missions, or should they become more narrowly focused?

How are Community College Missions Determined?

One of the most difficult tasks in addressing the missions of the community college is determining what they are, much less what they should be. This determination has been done in several different ways, with important consequences for how we view the community college.

Public Statements of Mission. One way to ascertain the community college's missions has been to rely on public statements by authoritative policymakers and community college leaders. These statements can take the form of state legislation or a state master plan laying out the functions of a state's community colleges. For example, Section 130.003 of the Texas Education Code states: "Texas public community colleges are two-year institutions whose primary mission is to serve their local taxing districts and service areas in Texas in offering vocational, technical, and academic courses for certification or associate degrees. Continuing education, remedial and compensatory education consistent with open admissions policies, and programs of counseling and guidance also are provided" (Texas College and University System, n.p.). These authoritative statements can also come from national associations—particularly the American Association of Community Colleges (AACC)—that speak on behalf of community colleges. For example, AACC (2004) has declared: "Community colleges are centers of educational opportunity . . . inclusive institutions that welcome all who desire to learn, regardless of wealth, heritage, or previous academic experience" (p. 1).

However, there are always two questions about these kinds of authoritative statements. Do they speak for all the constituents of the community college, or do they speak only for those who issue the statements? Similarly, do such statements capture what community colleges really do, or what they *should* do or *purport* to do? These questions have led to the use of other methods for mission determination.

Programmatic Offerings as Mission. A second method for determining the missions of the community college is to examine its *operations*. The institution's missions can be inferred from typical programmatic offerings, enrollment patterns, and organizational procedures. This, in fact, has been the preferred means of determining community college missions by community college scholars. Cohen and Brawer (2003), for example, organize their well-known textbook on the community college by the functions of the institution defined in terms of its major offerings: occupational education, collegiate and transfer education, remedial education, and adult and community education.

Bailey and Morest (2004) have developed another offerings-based schema, consisting of three dimensions. The first is the core, which is concerned with remediation and degree-granting programs leading to academic or occupational associate degrees. The second dimension, called the *vertical dimension,* involves relationships with high schools and four-year colleges, and focuses on traditional college-age students; it includes dual enrollment and Tech Prep, articulation with four-year institutions, the community college baccalaureate (CCB), and honors programs. Finally, the *horizontal* dimension includes noncredit contract training, continuing education, small business development, General Educational Development (GED) preparation, English as a Second Language, summer camps for children, and so forth.

Effects of Community Colleges. The third means of understanding the missions of the community college is to examine its *effects,* using institutional outcomes to draw out both overt and covert intentions and intended and unintended (but systematic) outcomes (Brint and Karabel, 1989; Dougherty, 1994). This has been a primary method used by critics of the community college, who doubt that the announced missions of the community college fully capture the institution's true purposes. These critics note that—whatever the announced mission—the fact remains that the majority of community colleges' many disadvantaged students do not receive a degree, and if they do, it carries a lower reward than a four-year degree. Moreover, students with baccalaureate aspirations who enter community colleges are statistically less likely to realize their ambitions than students similar in background, high school preparation, and aspirations who enter four-year colleges (Alfonso, forthcoming; Dougherty, 1994; Pascarella and Terenzini, 2005). The critics argue that these effects are not accidental but pervasive, a product of the community college's role in maintaining social inequality as well as providing college opportunity.

Forces Shaping Community College Missions

The community college is not a static institution and neither are its missions. They have changed over time, with new missions appearing and older ones changing in importance. The workforce and economic development mission appeared as early as the 1910s but really flowered only in the 1960s (Brint and Karabel, 1989; Dougherty, 1994). Similarly, the mission of providing adult education and community services emerged in the 1930s but did not command much attention until the 1970s (Ratcliffe, 1994). More recently, the long-standing mission of facilitating educational opportunity—particularly the pursuit of the bachelor's degree—has changed as several states (most notably Florida) have permitted community colleges to confer their own baccalaureate degrees (Floyd, 2005).

The changing composition and relative importance of certain missions in relation to others begs the question: What forces have shaped and will continue to shape the missions of the community college? Debate has swirled around the relative importance of factors external and internal to the community college, and within that, the relative importance and meaning of business demand. Certainly, external societal changes and demands have played an important role in shaping the community college's missions. For example, the rise of the workforce and economic development mission—focused on occupational education—is directly related to changes in the structure of the economy and rising demands for new skills from businesses and students.

Other scholars have pointed to the values and interests of government and community college officials in shaping the community college's missions (Brint and Karabel, 1989; Dougherty, 1994). These values—including facilitating educational opportunity and serving the needs of the community—have led government and community college officials to push for the development of adult education and community services (Mezack, 1994; Ratcliffe, 1994), and the right of community colleges to offer baccalaureates in certain applied fields (Floyd, 2005).

However, the self-interests of some government officials and community college leaders have also played an important role in the development of new community college missions. Government officials have supported the workforce and economic development function in good part as a means to enhance their own political popularity and electability by promoting economic growth. Meanwhile, community college leaders have supported workforce and economic development as a means of realizing various institutional interests, including establishing a distinct niche for the community college in higher education, cultivating support from business and governmental elites, and seeking new sources of revenue (Brint and Karabel, 1989; Dougherty, 1994; Dougherty and Bakia, 2000).

Similar institutional and self-interests may be at work in the support that government and community college officials have given to the growing role of the community college in baccalaureate provision in various states. For some state officials, the community college baccalaureate allows a greater number of students to earn a bachelor's degree at a lower cost. And for some community college officials, the development of baccalaureate programs not only serves the goal of furthering educational opportunity, but also an interest in gaining greater prestige for their institution.

Finally, any discussion of the forces shaping community college missions must acknowledge that community colleges differ greatly by geographic region. There are considerable variations across states—and even localities in the same state—in which missions community colleges emphasize. In some states, such as North Carolina, the community college is decidedly oriented toward occupational training; the transfer function has been a fairly recent development. Conversely, the transfer function has long been a very important mission of the Florida community colleges (Dougherty, Reid, and Nienhusser, 2006). However, even in that state there are big variations across community colleges in the extent of the transfer mission, with some colleges having over 80 percent of their associate of arts graduates transferring to one of the state universities within five years, and others having only 50 percent of them doing so (Florida Department of Education, 2001). These intrastate differences in the extent of the transfer mission may reflect how closely community colleges are located to four-year public colleges, as well as the nature of their particular local economy, demography, and polity.

Mission Compatibility and Conflict

The historical evolution of community college missions—particularly when they are products of conflicting interests—raises the question of how compatible those missions are. And in fact, a variety of analysts of the community college have noted that the institution's missions are frequently in conflict. We will first review these analyses and then take up the question of whether those conflicts are resolvable.

Sources of Mission Conflict. A general conflict between multiple missions lies in the simple fact that community colleges—like all organizations—have limited amounts of money, time, and energy; serving one mission may thus entail cutting into the resources available for others. But some observers have noted that mission conflict goes deeper. One of the main sources of mission conflict is an institution's emphasis on occupational education. Occupational education can be quite expensive, requiring community colleges to subsidize higher-cost occupational programs from the surpluses generated by less-expensive academic programs (Bailey and Morest, 2004; Morest, 2006). Moreover, an emphasis on occupational education may be associated with less institutional success in transfer. There is evidence that students who major in community college occupational programs are significantly less likely to transfer—net of differences in social background, high school preparation, and educational and occupational aspirations—than students who major in academic programs (Dougherty and Kienzl, 2006). However, other scholars argue that, once one controls for student characteristics, any negative effect of vocational emphasis on transfer rates disappears (Cohen and Brawer, 2003; Roksa, 2006).

The growing interest in the community college baccalaureate—although it has been applauded as enhancing the community college's mission to foster baccalaureate attainment (Dougherty, 1994)—has also been identified as a source of mission conflict. Some argue that the CCB may undercut the community college's transfer mission. Moreover, it may lead colleges to reduce their attention to occupational and remedial education (Bailey and Morest, 2004; Morest, 2006).

Finally, the growing interest in community college honors programs may be a source of mission conflict. It has been argued that as such programs grow, they undercut community colleges' commitment to seeking out less prepared (and therefore less advantaged) students. (For more on this topic, see Chapter Five in this volume.)

What to Do About Mission Conflict? In the face of mission conflict, some analysts in the 1980s argued that community colleges should narrow their missions, reducing or even eliminating some of them in order to focus more on others. Some called for eliminating the transfer function and concentrating instead on occupational education (Breneman and Nelson, 1981; Clowes and Levine, 1989). Others called for cutting back on occupational education and putting more emphasis on transfer education (Brint and Karabel, 1989; Dougherty, 1994). Although mission narrowing may make sense, it is unlikely to happen. One reason is that community colleges gain too much from a broad, multipurpose portfolio of functional missions. A broad portfolio allows the colleges to serve many different social interests, thus garnering widespread public and governmental support. It also buffers them from economic and political uncertainty. If one mission loses favor, other functional missions are in place to pick up the slack (Bailey and Morest, 2004; Dougherty, 1994).

Furthermore, even if community colleges narrowed the number of missions they emphasized, it is not clear that mission conflict would be eliminated, for it is also rooted in the essential contradictions of U.S. society. This is a society deeply divided by class, race, gender, and other factors. These divisions show up in the community college in debates about preserving open access while maintaining academic excellence and in conversations about meeting students' needs for broad-based occupational skills and employers' desires for skills more narrowly tailored to their particular interests. These contradictions have divided the community college almost from its inception, and will likely continue to do so, even if some institutions prioritize one mission over another (Dougherty, 1994).

But if mission breadth (and therefore conflict) is inescapable, this does not mean that institutions should ignore those conflicts and treat them as irresolvable. Community colleges can pursue certain strategies to ease mission conflict. For example, conflict between a strong emphasis on occupational education and an emphasis on transfer can be eased by working with four-year colleges and universities to make occupational credits as transferable as possible. By so doing, occupational students may be more likely to transfer, and will pay less of a penalty in terms of course repetition if they do. A number of states are encouraging articulation of applied associate of science degrees, and it is a development that should be strongly encouraged (Dougherty, Reid, and Nienhusser, 2006; Ignash and Kotun, 2005). Despite this and other developments, mission conflict will remain, and it is important that it be honestly acknowledged, rather than wished away.

Summary and Conclusions

In this chapter we have tried to show that the missions of the community college are complex and open to a variety of analytic approaches and substantive conclusions. The community college is a multivalent institution, pursuing many different and sometimes conflicting missions. Moreover, community college missions differ among geographic regions and the emphasis community colleges have placed on any particular mission has varied over time. Any analysis of the institution's missions must honor this complexity.

It is hard to forecast the future missions of the community college. The safest bet is to forecast little change, certainly in the short run. At this point, the community college is deeply institutionalized in the fabric of our higher education system and society, and therefore major changes are unlikely. Nonetheless, bellwethers of change are there. The transfer and baccalaureate missions of the community college are likely to get stronger in the coming years. More students will be pursuing the baccalaureate as the high school degree continues to lose worth and as the number of high school graduates rises by 5 percent between 2006 and 2010. But these baccalaureate aspirants will increasingly matriculate at community colleges because university tuitions are likely to continue to rise sharply, pricing out many students (Morest, 2006).

In addition, fiscal pressures faced by state governments will likely lead to slow growth in appropriations for community colleges. This will encourage the colleges to continue their avid search for new revenues (and therefore new missions), especially in the areas of workforce development and continuing education (see Chapters Six and Eight of this volume). Meanwhile, the weakening industrial base of the U.S. economy and growing outsourcing of industrial production from the United States has reduced corporate demand for contract training, but it is also leading community colleges to emphasize a high-skill "new vocationalism" that puts a premium on eventual attainment of the baccalaureate degree (see again Chapter Six).

A weakening economy is also likely to promote the remedial function of the community college. As more students enter higher education in search of an economic safety net, the higher education system will increasingly be working with students with lower levels of academic preparation and therefore greater need for remediation. Meanwhile, that same increase in student demand will allow public universities to continue their pursuit of admissions selectivity and to slough off remedial education on community colleges (Shaw, 2001).

References

Alfonso, M. "The Impact of Community College Attendance on Baccalaureate Attainment." *Research in Higher Education*, forthcoming.

American Association of Community Colleges. *About Community Colleges.* Washington, D.C.: American Association of Community Colleges, 2004. http://www.aacc.nche.edu/Template.cfm?section=AboutCommunityColleges. Accessed Jan. 3, 2006.

Bailey, T., and Morest, V. S. *The Organizational Efficiency of Multiple Missions for Community Colleges.* New York: Columbia University, Teachers College, Community College Research Center, 2004.

Bogart, Q. "The Community College Mission." In G. Baker (ed.), *A Handbook on the Community College in America.* Westport, Conn: Greenwood Press, 1994.

Breneman, D. W., and Nelson, S. C. *Financing Community Colleges.* Washington, D.C.: Brookings Institution, 1981.

Brint, S. G., and Karabel, J. B. *The Diverted Dream.* New York: Oxford University Press, 1989.

Clowes, D. A., and Levine, B. H. "Community, Technical, and Junior Colleges: Are They Leaving Higher Education?" *Journal of Higher Education*, 1989, *60*, 349–355.

Cohen, A. M., and Brawer, F. B. *The American Community College.* (4th ed.) San Francisco: Jossey-Bass, 2003.

Dougherty, K. J. *The Contradictory College.* Albany: State University of New York Press, 1994.

Dougherty, K. J., and Bakia, M. "Community Colleges and Contract Training." *Teachers College Record*, 2000, *102*(1), 197–243.

Dougherty, K. J., and Hong, E. "Performance Accountability as Imperfect Panacea: The Community College Experience." In T. Bailey and V. S. Morest (eds.), *Defending the Community College Equity Agenda.* Baltimore: Johns Hopkins University Press, 2006.

Dougherty, K. J., and Kienzl, G. S. "It's Not Enough to Get Through the Open Door: Inequalities by Social Background in Transfer from Community Colleges to Four-Year Colleges." *Teachers College Record*, 2006, *108*(3), 452–487.

Dougherty, K. J., Reid, M., and Nienhusser, H. K. "Five States of Policy: A Brief on Policies and Policy Needs in the First Five Achieving the Dream States." New York: Columbia University, Teachers College, Community College Research Center, 2006.

Florida Department of Education. *AA Transfers to the State University System* (Data Trends No. 23). Tallahassee: Florida Department of Education, 2001. http://www.fldoe.org/CC/OSAS/DataTrendsResearch/DT-23.pdf. Accessed Oct. 6, 2006.

Floyd, D. "The Community College Baccalaureate in the U.S." In D. Floyd, M. Skolnik, and K. Walker (eds.), *The Community College Baccalaureate.* Sterling, Va.: Stylus Press, 2005.

Ignash, J. M., and Kotun, D. "Results of a National Study of Transfer in Occupational/Technical Degrees: Policies and Practices." *Journal of Applied Research in the Community College*, 2005, *12*(2), 109–120

Mezack, M. "Synthesis of the Literature on the Community Services Function." In G. Baker (ed.), *A Handbook on the Community College in America.* Westport, Conn: Greenwood Press, 1994.

Morest, V. S. "Double Vision: How Balancing Multiple Missions Is Shaping the Future of the Community College." In T. Bailey and V. S. Morest (eds.), *Defending the Community College Equity Agenda.* Baltimore: Johns Hopkins University Press, 2006.

Pascarella, E. T., and Terenzini, P. T. *How College Affects Students.* (2nd ed.) San Francisco: Jossey-Bass, 2005.

Ratcliffe, J. L. "Seven Streams in the Historical Development of the Modern American Community College." In G. Baker (ed.), *A Handbook on the Community College in America.* Westport, Conn: Greenwood Press, 1994.

Roksa, J. "Does the Vocational Focus of Community Colleges Hinder Students' Educational Attainment?" *Review of Higher Education,* 2006, 29(4), 499–526.

Shaw, K. "Reframing Remediation as a Systemic Phenomenon." In B. K. Townsend and S. B. Twombly (eds.), *Community Colleges.* Norwood, N.J.: Ablex, 2001.

Texas College and University System. Supervision by Coordinating Board, 130.001 Texas Education Code, 1971.

KEVIN J. DOUGHERTY *is associate professor of higher education and senior research associate at the Community College Research Center at Teachers College, Columbia University.*

BARBARA K. TOWNSEND *is professor of higher and continuing education at the University of Missouri-Columbia and a former community college faculty member and administrator.*

2

America's community colleges have a unique mission to provide open access and affordable education to all who desire to learn. Unfortunately, this core mission is being threatened by myriad economic, social, and political challenges that community college leaders must confront and overcome.

A Case for the Community College's Open Access Mission

Henry D. Shannon, Ronald C. Smith

Of all the developments in American higher education, few have had a greater impact than the creation of the egalitarian mission of community, technical, and junior colleges. These institutions' shared commitment to access is as American as the Declaration of Independence. The American Association of Community Colleges (1998) defines the role and scope of the community college in this way:

> The network of community, technical, and junior colleges in America is unique and extraordinarily successful. It is, perhaps, the only sector of higher education that truly can be called a "movement," one in which the members are bound together and inspired by common goals. From the very first, these institutions, often called "the people's colleges," have stirred an egalitarian zeal among their members. The open door policy has been pursued with an intensity and dedication comparable to the populist, civil rights, and feminist crusades. While more elitist institutions may define excellence as exclusion, community colleges have sought excellence in service to the many. [p. 5]

Community college faculty and staff know firsthand how community colleges "expand minds and change lives every day" (St. Louis Community College, 2006). Community college faculty are not judged by their research or publishing but on the strength of their ability to help students learn and to engage students with different backgrounds, ethnicities, and aspirations.

NEW DIRECTIONS FOR COMMUNITY COLLEGES, no. 136, Winter 2006 © 2006 Wiley Periodicals, Inc.
Published online in Wiley InterScience (www.interscience.wiley.com) • DOI: 10.1002/cc.255

The community colleges' proverbial *open door,* which ensures access for all who can benefit, is the foundation on which all other community college operations rest. The open door concept influences admissions and enrollment processes, curricular structures, faculty hiring, the relationships between community colleges and four-year institutions, advising and counseling activities, and colleges' responses to the needs of the K–12 sector, as well as those of the local economy. Indeed, the open door concept is critical to our understanding of the community college itself.

Why the Open Door Mission Is Vital

Evidence of the importance of and the necessity for the open access mission abounds. Nationally, community colleges enroll 47 percent of black undergraduate students, 56 percent of Hispanic undergraduates, 48 percent of Asian/Pacific Islanders, and 58 percent of Native American students (American Association of Community Colleges, 2006). Because so many of these students come from low-income or educationally disadvantaged backgrounds, one can infer that without the open door, few would be able to attend an institution of higher education.

The number of high school graduates in the United States has increased greatly over the past twenty years, and analysts anticipate an additional 10 percent increase between 2001 and 2014 (Hussar, 2005). This projection, combined with the poor academic accomplishments of many high school graduates, makes the open door a critical community college mission. Until high schools adequately prepare all students for success in college, the open door is imperative.

However, recent high school graduates are not the only student population for whom the open door is critical. Many community college students are adults (defined here as twenty-six to thirty-five years old) who must attend college to maintain their jobs, acquire a job, or earn a promotion. For quite a few years, the average age of community college students was twenty-nine (American Association of Community Colleges, 2006). Although more recent data (Adelman, 2004) indicate that the median age is closer to twenty-four, it is still higher than that of students at many four-year schools, which are much more likely to enroll recent high school graduates. Preserving the open door is essential for these older students who require flexibility in course offerings, low cost, and proximity to their work or home.

Parallel to the open door mission is the commitment to providing quality education at an affordable cost. Although community college tuition and fees have increased over the years in response to economic conditions and state and local tax policies, the average price of attending a community college is lower than that of a four-year college, and has not increased at the same rate as tuition and fees at four-year institutions. Average annual tuition and fees at community colleges for in-state students in 1976–77 were $283 (in current dollars). By 2000–01, that had risen to $1,359, an increase of

NEW DIRECTIONS FOR COMMUNITY COLLEGES • DOI: 10.1002/cc

380 percent. During the same time period, however, average annual in-state tuition and fees at public four-year colleges rose from $617 to $3,506, an increase of 468 percent (Kasper, 2002). Without low tuition and fees, many community college students would be denied access to higher education.

Because of their open door, community colleges have acted as gateways to higher education for many Americans; this mission is more important now than ever before. We live today in an age in which the key strategic resource for success is knowledge. As Friedman (2005) contends, societies that can extend knowledge to all segments of the population will become the new world leaders. Therefore, community colleges must retain and strengthen their mission of inclusion in order to prepare more knowledgeable citizens.

Threats to the Open Access Mission

The community college's open access mission is being threatened by several challenges, including geographic accessibility, demographic shifts, fiscal constraints, and a variety of other issues. George Boggs (2004), president of the American Association of Community Colleges, calls these various challenges "the perfect storm" (p. 8). He states, "Despite such highly visible public support, the nation's community colleges now face unprecedented challenges. In the past three years, student enrollment pressure has escalated and college leaders have struggled to meet demand in the face of steep budget cuts, limited facilities, faculty turnover, rising technology costs, and increasing numbers of students who need remedial work before they can take college-level classes" (p. 8).

Financial challenges in particular threaten the open access mission. Community colleges in states like California, which has over 2.5 million community college students, are being asked to do more with less. Furthermore, community colleges in states like New York—where in 2005 four-year colleges and universities refused admission to 38 percent of transfer applicants—face the possibility that students seeking to transfer to four-year public institutions may not be accepted because of lack of space (Boulard, 2006).

The level of federal support for community colleges also threatens the open door mission. Recently, the administration of George W. Bush proposed a Higher Education Act amendment that would decrease funding for community colleges that do not meet externally imposed benchmarks of student retention and graduation. Because many community college students enter the institution for short-term training that does not lead to a degree or certificate, and because many others attend sporadically or part-time in order to support their families or raise children, this amendment would dramatically decrease funding for community colleges. To maintain existing revenues, community colleges would be forced to curtail admission of all students not likely to meet federally imposed retention and graduation expectations, or would have to significantly raise tuition and fees to cover the loss of federal and state funding. These and other proposed policies would effectively close the open door and limit the community college's ability to provide access to higher education to all who desire to learn.

We should understand that when state and federal governments make policies that reduce amounts of need-based aid, there is a disproportionate effect on community college students, who are arguably some of the most economically disadvantaged of all college going students. Loans have become the aid-of-the-day for most low-income students since the reduction of need-based aid began more than twenty years ago (Strauss, 2001). Although it is true that both rich and poor borrow money to attend college, a higher percentage of low-income students borrow, and borrowing has been shown to be a greater burden on low-income families. "Prospective students from low-income families, and those who would be the first in their families to attend college, may be inhibited from enrolling by fear of high debt. . . . [L]ow-income students are more likely than other students to be contributing to the support of their families while attending college" (National Center for Public Policy and Higher Education, 2002, p. 7). One should also note that community colleges suffer more from state budget cuts than four-year colleges and universities because community colleges rely more on state appropriations than their four-year counterparts. Four-year colleges and universities can mitigate budget cuts by tapping into other revenue resources, such as federal research grants, alumni contributions, and higher tuition paid by out-of-state students.

The predicaments caused by reduced allocations in two states may be instructive here. In California, almost 50 percent of the money spent by the community college system comes from the state, compared with 25 percent of the amount spent by the University of California. Thus, the $135.5 million cut that the university suffered as a result of the 2003 budget cuts amounted to a 1 percent reduction in the system's total funds. In contrast, the $285 million cut in spending for the two-year college system equaled about 6 percent of its budget (Hebel, 2003).

Similarly, the lawmakers in Washington cut appropriations for the University of Washington's Seattle campus by 8.6 percent in fiscal year 2004, while also approving a reduction of 3.8 percent for nearby Seattle Central Community College. However, because 63 percent of Seattle Central's support is derived from the state, compared with only 13.4 percent of the University of Washington's, the actual cuts accounted for 2.4 percent of the community college's budget and only 1.2 percent of the university's budget (Hebel, 2003). Such cuts are of concern because they affect student enrollment. According to Dr. Charles H. Mitchell, now the chancellor of the Seattle Community College system, "the budget cuts hurt neediest students the most" (Hebel, 2003, p. 2). The financial pressures forced Mitchell to consider cutting from programs like adult basic education and English as a Second Language, whose students typically do not pay tuition. The programmatic cuts significantly hurt the college's ability to serve the large population of refugees from East Africa and Southeast Asia who live in the community and rely on the college for training.

Many states have also reduced their allocations for community colleges because of the imbalance of revenues and expenditures and the laws that give preference to K–12 education. The competition for state funds has become a veritable battle, with all state agencies vying for a more limited pool of funds. Furthermore, many citizens are not as willing as in the past to agree to tax increases; thus, community colleges have been forced to raise tuition to balance their books. This deadly combination of shrinking state resources and increased tuition has placed a heavy burden on those students whom the community college is designed to serve.

Strengthening the Open Door Mission

We believe that the community college mission of providing an open door to higher education must be strengthened. How can this be done? To begin with, community college, political, and community leaders must accept the realities that come with operating an open access institution. In particular, community colleges will have to reaffirm their commitment to providing remedial education for the large numbers of high school graduates who have not mastered the basic skills of reading, writing, mathematics, and computers. We are not just talking about appending a developmental program to existing academic divisions, but creating autonomous organizational units with an accompanying budget and staff in order to addresses student underpreparedness and remediation in a holistic manner.

Such an organizational unit might include orientation courses that help students understand the nature of college-level work and gain the knowledge and skills that are required to succeed in college. Course content might include how to study, how to get help from experts when needed, how to understand that taking moderate risks is necessary for success, and how to think realistically about accomplishing one's goals. For example, many community college students are juggling family obligations and full- or part-time jobs; these students probably should not attempt to enroll in a full course load. These lessons must be imparted to students in conjunction with the remedial courses in English and math required to ensure their success. Faculty who teach in such a remedial unit need to be trained in effective developmental teaching methods, and must learn how to address underprepared students' unique needs and challenges.

Furthermore, advocacy and support organizations such as the American Association of Community Colleges and the League for Innovation in the Community College must redouble their efforts to promote the community college as the most effective and efficient vehicle for filling society's need for an educated populace and a world-class workforce. There exist ample statistics, demographic projections, economic information, and success stories about community colleges to support these arguments. We suspect that community college advocates and personnel spend too much time preaching to the choir instead of attempting to influence those who control funding and

New Directions for Community Colleges • DOI: 10.1002/cc

those who make policies. College leaders should emphasize the enormous need in the United States to make sure we are educating those minority and low-income groups whose knowledge and skills are essential to the betterment of our own society. The very success of the global competitiveness of the United States is at stake.

Conclusion

If there is one overarching concept that defines the community college, it is the open door mission. Recently, Dr. Mary Fifield (2006), president of Bunker Hill Community College, addressed this issue before the Secretary of Education's Commission on the Future of Higher Education. Dr. Fifield stated: "Community colleges are a uniquely American invention. From their start as junior colleges in the early 1900s, these two-year institutions signaled a dramatic change that expanded educational opportunity from only the affluent to include the poorest and most disadvantaged among us" (p. 1). The results speak for themselves. Today's community colleges educate millions of first-generation college students, minorities, women, and students with remedial needs. We strongly assert that the community college must live out its access mission in order for our nation to reach its full potential.

References

Adelman, C. *Principal Indicators of Student Academic Histories in Postsecondary Education, 1972–2000.* Washington, D.C.: U.S. Department of Education, 2004.

American Association of Community Colleges, Commission on the Future of the Community Colleges. *Building Communities: A Vision for a New Century.* Washington, D.C.: American Association of Community Colleges, 1998.

American Association of Community Colleges. *Fast Facts.* Washington D.C.: American Association of Community Colleges, 2006. http://www.aacc.nche.edu/Content/NavigationMenu/AboutCommunityColleges/Fast_Facts1/Fast_Facts.htm. Accessed Aug. 7, 2006.

Boggs, G. "In a Perfect Storm." *Change,* Nov.-Dec. 2004, p. 8.

Boulard, G. "Transferring to Universities in N.Y. May Get Harder If Budget Passes." *Community College Week,* Feb. 13, 2006, pp. 3, 8.

Fifield, M. "Testimony on Behalf of the American Association of Community Colleges." Testimony prepared for the Secretary of Education's Commission on the Future of Higher Education, Boston, Mar. 20, 2006. http://www.aacc.nche.edu/Template.cfm?Section=Testimony&template=/ContentManagement/ContentDisplay.cfm&ContentID=16111&InterestCategoryID=211&Name=Testimony&ComingFrom=InterestDisplay. Accessed Aug. 7, 2006.

Friedman, T. *The World Is Flat: A Brief History of the Twenty-First Century.* New York: Farrar, Straus and Giroux, 2005.

Hebel, S. "Community Colleges Face Disproportionate Cuts in State Budgets." *Chronicle of Higher Education,* 2003, 49(38), 2. http://chronicle.com/free/v49/i38a02101.htm. Accessed June 23, 2006.

Hussar, W. J. *Projection of Education Statistics to 2014* (NCES 2005–074). Washington, D.C.: U.S. Department of Education, 2005.

Kasper, H. T. "The Changing Role of the Community College." *Occupational Outlook Quarterly*, Winter 2002, pp. 1–8.

National Center for Public Policy and Higher Education. "Losing Ground: A National Status Report on the Affordability of Higher Education." San Jose, Calif.: National Center for Public Policy and Higher Education, 2002. http://www.highereducation.org/reports/losing_ground/ar.shtml. Accessed Aug. 10, 2006.

St. Louis Community College. "Mission." St. Louis, Mo.: St. Louis Community College, 2006. http://www.stlcc.cc.mo.us/about/mission.html. Accessed Aug. 10, 2006.

Strauss, L. *Trends in Community College Financing: Challenges of the Past, Present and Future* (ERIC Digest No. EDO-JC-10). Los Angeles: University of California, Los Angeles, ERIC Clearinghouse for Community Colleges, 2001.

HENRY D. SHANNON is chancellor of St. Louis Community College, Missouri, and a past board chair of the American Association of Community Colleges.

RONALD C. SMITH is former acting president and retired emeritus executive dean of St. Louis Community College at Forest Park, Missouri.

3

Educating for civic competence is an important societal mission of the community college. This chapter describes obstacles to and opportunities for the success of this mission.

Appraising the Efficacy of Civic Education at the Community College ⟨⟨ Missions :

George H. Higginbottom, Richard M. Romano • Workforce Training
• Baccalaureate Transfer

Community colleges have multiple missions. The two most visible and vocal are the occupational education and workforce training mission and the baccalaureate transfer mission. The former resonates deeply with community leaders and provides rich justification for financial support. Success in this mission is a potent measure of institutional effectiveness. The baccalaureate transfer function, aimed at moving graduates along to academic majors and career programs at four-year institutions, is of equal importance. However, it seems indisputable to us that a major societal function of higher education—to provide general (as civic) education—is an equally important measure of the community college's performance and value. The arguments that follow are predicated on three propositions: (1) the provision of general education is more a public good than a private one; (2) civic competence has historically been the essence of general education's public purpose; and (3) effective general education needs to be cross-curricular and integrative.

Not all community college general education goals are, or ought to be, explicitly civic. However, we contend that education for civic competence has been and continues to be the principal public purpose of general education—herein referred to as "general (as civic)" education. From Thomas Jefferson's vision of education to "inform the discretion" of a democratic citizenry, to Dewey's seminal study of the democratic ends of public education in *Democracy and Education* (1916), to numerous contemporary advocates espousing similar rationales (Ehrlich, 2000, for example), the overarching

NEW DIRECTIONS FOR COMMUNITY COLLEGES, no. 136, Winter 2006 © 2006 Wiley Periodicals, Inc.
Published online in Wiley InterScience (www.interscience.wiley.com) • DOI: 10.1002/cc.256

societal goal of education, both secondary and postsecondary, has been civic competence.

In this chapter we shall assume that the community college is indeed effective in educating students for both successful employment and baccalaureate transfer. Further, we claim that the general education curriculum, in particular its contributions to effective democratic citizenship education, advances a critically important societal goal. How optimally it might do that, and the obstacles and opportunities that it faces in trying to do so, are the issues that frame our discussion.

The Goals of General (as Civic) Education

There is a consensus in higher education on the learning that graduates ought to hold in common. This learning is usually called *general education,* an ensemble of skills, knowledge, and dispositions that partially make up the attributes that we associate with an educated person: one who, in the parlance of Progressive Era educators, is able to make sense of experience, personal and vicarious, current and historical (Miller, 1988). This education derives principally from the content of the arts and sciences disciplines and their unique modes of inquiry, and is customarily organized by subject and method into clusters—science, mathematics, social science, and humanities.

Although liberal arts transfer programs usually have enough room to incorporate the civic education component of general education, occupational and vocational education curricula are typically too crowded to incorporate more than a few arts and sciences courses, and even these are often turned to vocational ends. Therefore, robust civic education programs that propose to include all students, while being adequately responsive to societal expectations for developing educated citizens, must be infused into existing courses and cocurricular activities across the community college campus. These efforts also must be carefully conceived, deployed, and assessed; doing so presupposes clear and widespread understanding as to what needs to be taught and in which venues.

Among the desired attributes of *liberally educated* college graduates, held to be outcomes of arts and sciences course work, are intellectual curiosity; broad knowledge; inquiry, literacy, and critical-thinking and problem-solving skills; enriched sensibility leading to the capacity for empathy; and a moral point of view that respects human and public affairs. Although not as clearly applicable as vocational and professional skills and knowledge, the attainment of a liberal education is also practical because it undergirds the capabilities that individuals must acquire to be successful in the economic, social, and political aspects of their private and public lives, and especially in their lives as democratic citizens.

The importance of the civic education mission was recognized in the Truman Commission Report of 1947, widely regarded as providing a major stimulus to the modern community college movement. However, as the community college grappled with rapid sector and institutional growth during the 1960s and 1970s, the citizenship education goals so vigorously advocated in this report—and the courses that served those ends—were subordinated to the narrower workplace training goals of the emerging vocational programs. (For a detailed history, see Higginbottom, 1991.)

Beginning in the late 1970s and continuing through the 1990s came a resurgence of interest in reforming the largely shattered general education core at both the four-year and the two-year college. Harvard's *Report on the Core Curriculum* (Faculty of Arts and Sciences, 1978), the revamping of the curriculum at Miami Dade Community College (Lukenbill and McCabe, 1978), the urgings of higher education organizations such as the American Association of Community Colleges, the American Association for Higher Education, the Association for the Study of Higher Education, and the work of Boyer and Levine (1981), Gaff (1983), and Cohen and Brawer (1987), helped spawn a national debate over the value and purposes of general education. These attempts to restore some coherence to the general education core and return it to its base in liberal learning were at least partially successful at the community college level (Higginbottom and Romano, 1995). Still, the public aims of the community college have a weak footing and are often subordinated to workplace utility goals (Higginbottom, 1994). If education for citizenship is to be a responsibility of the nation's community colleges, what might we expect such a program to look like?

A Generic Community College Civic Education Program

Unattainable through course work alone, civic education requires a deliberate, integrative program of skill development, theoretical understanding, and practice. Because civic competence is so multidimensional, it must be a collegewide goal: an integrated program of course, curricular, and cocurricular elements, framed by the institutional mission and vigorously supported by college administrators, faculty, and staff. Student accretion of citizenship competencies will depend ultimately on the faculty's understanding of the constitutive features of civic education and a willingness to incorporate goals and pertinent teaching strategies into their instruction, as well as their active support of cross-curricular and cocurricular programs and activities. Substantial in-service education and training will be essential, as will imaginative and dedicated leadership at all levels of the institution.

A successful campuswide civic education program would include course work in U.S. history and other social sciences, including public policy study and debate; possibly a capstone course that addresses development of an ethical perspective; a cocurricular civic forum conceived and managed by faculty and students; community service infusion programs;

and community public affairs and political forums. Foundational literacy skills—reading, writing, critical analysis, and discursive skills—while not always civic-specific, are other crucial elements of civic education that students would be required to learn and practice.

This is not to say that such a model would succeed fully in its aspirations. However, this model puts many of the requisite elements of civic education into place, and would need only a strong institutional commitment to ensure its effectiveness. Whether any institution can make such a commitment and follow through on it is quite another matter. Yet if we assume, for the sake of argument, that a general (as civic) education plan with the features just noted is in place, and that it is a well-understood program that is supported across the institution, we can begin to consider the likelihood of its success, given the various obstacles to realizing our cross-curricular infusion goal.

Obstacles and Opportunities in Implementing a Successful General (as Civic) Education Program

As we enter the twenty-first century, a familiar set of pressures threatens the goals of liberal and general education in the community college. Yet a few promising signs are also on the horizon. Which forces will be the most powerful is an open question. The best that we can do is highlight the current obstacles to and opportunities for implementing a successful general and civic education program and suggest what might be done to keep it alive and well.

Obstacles. There are a variety of obstacles to the general education mission, including the workforce training culture, demands for institutional accountability, the current mix of full- and part-time students and faculty, and shifting political agendas. All of these threaten to turn back the gains that general education made in the late twentieth century.

Workforce Training Culture. The niche that the community college has carved out for itself in higher education is associated with workforce training, both through formal degree programs, and increasingly, through short-term, nondegree programs directed at developing specific workplace skills. These programs emphasize the development of personal and *private* goods as opposed to the *public* ones we stress. Of course, there is nothing inherently wrong with this part of the community college mission. However, if it dominates the whole culture of the college, it may threaten the goals of general (as civic) education. In particular, many faculty in occupational areas will regard the community college's civic mission as a distraction. Pressure from them and the workforce side of the college, for instance, might lead to the substitution of technical writing for the more traditional English composition courses that emphasize critical thinking and self-expression. Similarly, public speaking, which is more of a personal and private good, will be substituted for competence in civic discourse, which has a public aim.

In addition, with the emphasis on preparing students to work, basic literacy in the form of remedial education may crowd out those subjects designed to deliver liberal learning. On the whole, the workforce training culture and general (as civic) education are uneasy bedfellows, and colleges will have to struggle to make them complementary.

Accountability. Colleges are rightfully being called upon to be accountable, and if they are not, their accreditation and funding may be jeopardized. Assessing broad societal goals such as civic competence, however, is difficult because such competencies are not always course-specific and include noncourse elements. Most colleges are working with outcomes-based competencies in order to meet demands for accountability, but the goals of integrative general education are not so easily adapted to the outcomes format. Assessing the value-added in critical thinking, for example, is more difficult than testing for competencies in accounting, engineering, or nursing. Even at the course level, evaluating learning through performance is difficult at best in an area like literature, where student-constructed meaning—not authors' plots and characters—is the paramount goal. Similarly, in history, where the primary instructional goal is historical understanding, not mere factual recall, technical assessment models can subvert faculty's views of worthwhile knowledge and learning. Along with the workforce development movement, the drive for accountability threatens to push liberal education into the background and substitute a narrow functionalist outlook.

The Changing Nature of the Student Body. Much has been written about the shifting demographics in the community college student population. What we focus on here is the part-time, full-time mix of students. In the past, circumstances have greatly increased the number of part-time or non-degree-seeking students, and this makes it more difficult to achieve the goals of general education. The current swirl of students between two- and four-year colleges results in more community college students transferring before they get degrees than afterward (Adelman, 1999; Townsend, 2000; Romano and Wisniewski, 2005). Moreover, students use the community college in different ways. If a four-year student attends a community college for a summer or a semester before returning to the four-year campus, is the community college responsible for that student's general (as civic) education? The answer to that question is *no!* A well-designed civic education program spread over two years will have little impact on the students enrolled for just one course. This situation, however, becomes part of the justification for infusing civic learning throughout the college. The occasional student will not receive the full treatment, but some elements can still be delivered. However, if the student body is populated by more part-time and occasional students, it is more difficult for the community college to achieve the goals of general and civic education. It also weakens the arguments of those who push for more ambitious general education programming.

The students themselves are also an obstacle, because most of them do not seem to value the goals of general education. Even four-year college students put more importance on workplace skills than citizenship skills. As Schneider and Humphreys (2005) have recently pointed out, proponents of the value of liberal and general education have not done a very good job of selling its importance to students and their parents. In the current student-as-consumer environment, this does not bode well for the future.

The Changing Nature of the Faculty and Power Over the Curriculum. Without question, the part-time, full-time mix of faculty also affects the goals of general and civic education. On this issue, economic constraints have clearly tilted the scale in favor of more part-time faculty at both two- and four-year colleges. Who is going to conceive, organize, administer, and assess the civic education infusion program? Part-time faculty are less able to influence the overall direction of the curriculum, and with fewer full-time faculty to carry the load, power over what is taught in a program shifts to college administrators. Community college administrators travel in the company of local employers and politicians. For administrators, it takes a deep commitment to the goals of common learning to resist the pressures of always meeting workplace needs. This means that employers and business advisory groups will have more influence over what is taught, and will be tempted to invade the general education core for their own purposes. In the end, the group that gains control of the curriculum will determine the nature of the general education program on each campus.

Political Winds. Much has been written about the impact of the so-called culture wars on the college curriculum (Higginbottom and Romano, 2001). The struggle for control and residual antagonisms can politicize the campus or state and local education hierarchies, and may blow the civic education agenda off course. For instance, civic education advocates might be accused by campus liberals of inculcating blind patriotism, a practice far from the critical and deliberative civic competence that we envision. Alternatively, conservative leaders, fearing a 1960s-type radical resurgence on campuses, may seek to throttle the development of participatory civic education by restricting general education requirements to the mastery of basic skills and discipline distributions.

Opportunities. Despite the threats that could compromise the objectives of general and civic education at the community college, some interesting opportunities exist for advancing it. Some of these, such as service learning, learning communities, and integrated studies, are internal to the college and are well under way. Others, such as the need for a flexible labor force in the age of changing technology and the global economy, are external forces that might affect the nature of the curriculum.

Flexibility of Faculty. Compared with faculty at the university level, those teaching in the arts and sciences at the community colleges are less bound to their discipline. Because they teach courses that are largely at a freshman or sophomore level, these community college faculty tend to be generalists rather than specialists. Arguably, they also think more about the process of teaching and learning than do university faculty. Doing so makes them more amenable to developing curricula and teaching strategies that emphasize integrated studies and involve students in the learning process. All of these factors favor the infusion of the broader goals of general education and civic competence into a variety of existing courses and new interdisciplinary courses and activities.

Service Learning and Learning Communities. In the past few years, community colleges have embraced learning communities and service learning as ways to engage students in the learning process. Service learning is the workshop of civic education. It brings some excitement to learning and helps students connect abstract ideas to practical concerns. To assist colleges in this effort, the American Association of Community Colleges has provided grant funding to support the goals of civic education and service learning on the campus level (Gottlieb and Robinson, 2002).

Learning communities also hold the promise of helping all students integrate their learning, an important goal of liberal and general education. When courses that are linked together are infused with elements of civic education, they can advance the goals that we are advocating. Used as a method for teaching remedial students, learning communities also hold the promise of bringing those who are underprepared for college-level work into the mainstream of the intellectual life of the campus (Grubb, 1999).

However, although both the service learning and the learning community movements have the promise of assisting faculty in advancing a civic education agenda, they will need to reach a much greater segment of the student population than they currently do in order to have a real impact on the overall culture of the college.

An Increased Market Demand for Broad-Based Education. Employers of technical and vocational graduates deliver a confusing message to students. Executives speak in public about the need for broad-based skills, but those who do the actual hiring look for industry-specific skills. At some point, the rhetoric of the executives may reach down to the hiring level, and the general education competencies that we are advocating will become more valued. On this point, the current debate over the outsourcing of American jobs is instructive.

Whether one thinks that outsourcing is a boon or a bane for the American worker, the controversy has people talking about the ways technology and globalization are transforming the U.S. economy. An important part of the message that students are receiving from the media and their parents is that they must become part of the knowledge society, which places a high value on going to college and engaging in lifelong learning. In addition, "flexibility and mobility are the watchwords of the new economy; a career spent with the same employer, or even in the same line of work, is fast becoming the exception

People are changing careers!

rather than the rule. Accordingly, students are now advised that the knowledge they gain in their majors will not be useful for long unless coupled with the skills and dispositions that enhance their ability to find and take advantage of new opportunities as they arise" (Huber and Hutchings, 2004, p. 2).

Uncertainty about the future has the potential to force students to take an interest in public affairs and to think about the impact of external forces on their private and public lives. In an age of increasing credentialism, it is also likely that greater numbers will become convinced that they should complete the associate degree and aspire to a bachelor's degree or beyond. Their doing so is likely to increase the demand for broad-based education and advance the civic agenda.

As for community college presidents and faculty, they are currently presented with conflicting messages. In one ear they hear the voices of the local business community and the workforce side of the campus about the importance of training students for a specific job in a specific industry. In the other ear they hear the voices of the futurists, saying, "Teach students how to think critically and creatively, teach them how to get along with people of other cultures, and give them broad-based skills that are transferable." Imparting these broad-based skills to students will make them better workers, to be sure, but also advance the goals of general education and produce better citizens. Community college leaders who think seriously about the future will need to pay less attention to those who advocate the narrow road.

Increased Emphasis on Transfer. Under the "Obstacles" heading, we suggested that a greater number of part-time, nondegree students would make the job of promoting general and civic education at the community college more difficult. If the opposite occurred, however, and the student population shifted in favor of the more traditional full-time student who was interested in attaining the bachelor's degree, then advancing the liberal education agenda would be easier. There are signs on the horizon that point to the likelihood of this scenario. For example, if the trend to cut state funding for public universities continues, public four-year colleges will increasingly privatize themselves by raising tuition and fees closer to the level of the private sector. For a larger number of students, going away to a four-year college will become too expensive, so they will attend the local community college for the first two years. In this unfortunate scenario, students are diverted from their first-choice college and the transfer population explodes. Of course, some of this is already occurring, but is it a short-term blip on the radar screen or a long-term trend? If the transfer population at the community college continues to grow rapidly, it will not only alter the composition of the student population and the types of courses offered to meet their needs but will also alter the composition of the community college faculty. Hence, more liberally trained and relatively fewer vocational faculty will be hired. With a greater voice at the table in curriculum discussions, the case for general and civic education will be strengthened.

NEW DIRECTIONS FOR COMMUNITY COLLEGES • DOI: 10.1002/cc

Conclusion

Will the forces generated by the threats to compromise civic education at the community college overwhelm those generated by the opportunities to expand it? Time will tell. But the net impact will differ depending on the mission of the college and the state in which it operates. It will also depend on the leadership in the colleges themselves. To keep liberal learning and the civic education mission alive and well, faculty must immerse themselves in developing the pedagogical skills that will advance these goals. Administrators must agree to hire more faculty who espouse these goals, and must guard the general education core from the pressures of the workplace test. Even at the most technical of colleges, general and civic education must be given a seat at the table.

References

Adelman, C. *Answers in the Tool Box: Academic Intensity, Attendance Patterns, and Bachelor's Degree Attainment.* Washington, D.C.: U.S. Department of Education, Office of Educational Research and Improvement, 1999.

Boyer, E. L. and Levine, A. *A Quest for Common Learning: The Aims of General Education.* Princeton, N.J.: Carnegie Foundation for the Advancement of Teaching, 1981.

Cohen, A. M., and Brawer, F. W. *The Collegiate Function of Community Colleges.* San Francisco: Jossey-Bass, 1987.

Dewey, J. *Democracy and Education: An Introduction to the Philosophy of Education.* New York: Macmillan, 1916.

Ehrlich, T. (ed.). *Civic Responsibility and Higher Education.* Washington, D.C.: American Council on Education/Oryx Press, 2000.

Faculty of Arts and Sciences. *Report on the Core Curriculum.* Cambridge, Mass.: Harvard University, Office of the Dean, Faculty of Arts and Sciences, 1978.

Gaff, J. G. *General Education Today.* San Francisco: Jossey-Bass, 1983.

Gottlieb, K., and Robinson, G. *A Practical Guide for Integrating Civic Responsibility into the Curriculum.* Washington, D.C.: Community College Press, 2002.

Grubb, W. N. *Honored but Invisible: An Inside Look at Teaching in Community Colleges.* New York: Routledge, 1999.

Higginbottom, G. *The Civic Ground of Collegiate General Education and the Community College.* Unpublished doctoral dissertation, Cornell University, 1991.

Higginbottom, G. "Workplace Utility and the Humanities: General and Occupational Education in the Community College." *Journal of General Education,* 1994, *43*(4), 273–288.

Higginbottom, G., and Romano, R. M. (eds.). *Curriculum Models for General Education.* New Directions for Community Colleges, no. 92. San Francisco: Jossey-Bass, 1995.

Higginbottom, G., and Romano, R. M. "SUNY General Education Reform and the Community Colleges: A Case Study in Cross-Purposes." In B. Townsend and S. Twombly (eds.), *Community Colleges: Policy in the Future Context.* Norwood, N.J.: Ablex, 2001.

Huber, M. T., and Hutchings, P. *Integrative Learning: Mapping the Terrain.* Washington, D.C.: Association of American Colleges and Universities, 2004.

Lukenbill, J. D., and McCabe, R. H. *General Education in a Changing Society.* Dubuque, Iowa: Kendall/Hunt, 1978.

Miller, G. *The Meaning of General Education: The Emergence of a Paradigm.* New York: Teachers College Press, 1988.

Romano, R. M., and Wisniewski, M. "Tracking Community College Transfers Using National Student Clearinghouse Data" (AIR Professional File, No. 94). Tallahassee, Fla.: Association for Institutional Research, 2005.

Schneider, C. G., and Humphreys, D. "Putting Liberal Education on the Radar Screen." *Chronicle of Higher Education*, 2005, 52(5), B20.

Townsend, B. K. "Transfer Students' Institutional Attendance Patterns: A Case Study." *College and University Journal*, 2000, 76(1), 21–24.

GEORGE H. HIGGINBOTTOM is retired dean of liberal arts at Broome Community College in Binghamton, New York.

RICHARD M. ROMANO is director of the Institute for Community College Research at Broome Community College, and a research associate at the Institute for Community College Development at Cornell University in Ithaca, New York.

NEW DIRECTIONS FOR COMMUNITY COLLEGES • DOI: 10.1002/cc

4

One of the original missions of the two-year college, the transfer mission was highly criticized in the latter part of the twentieth century. It is currently experiencing both challenges and opportunities due to changing enrollment demographics and governmental interest in transfer and articulation.

The Transfer Mission: Tried and True, But Troubled?

Barbara K. Townsend, Kristin B. Wilson

The community college is unique in its curricular transfer mission. Alone among institutions of higher education, the community college officially prepares students to transfer to four-year colleges and universities by providing the first two years of a bachelor's degree. This mission was a primary, but not the only, reason for the development of the two-year college. The college has also always provided career education, sometimes referred to as vocational or occupational-technical education. In recent years increasing numbers of community college students have chosen to enter these programs, designed to prepare them for immediate entry into the workplace rather than lead immediately to transfer. In the early 1960s, 26 percent of total enrollments in two-year colleges were in terminal occupational programs; by 1975, it was 35 percent (Cohen and Brawer, 2003), and currently it is over 50 percent. The extent of enrollment in vocational programs varies greatly by state, partly because of state-mandated foci for two-year colleges. However, across the nation, only 49 percent of the degrees awarded by community colleges in 2001–02 were in liberal arts and sciences, general studies, and humanities; 51 percent were in vocationally oriented fields such as business management and administrative services, and health professions and related sciences (Phillippe and Sullivan, 2005).

Consequently, some believe that the transfer mission, with its focus on the liberal arts, is at risk. For several decades, critics have charged that some students, particularly those from low socioeconomic backgrounds, were being tracked into vocational programs and away from transfer programs

(Karabel, 1972; Zwerling, 1976). Transfer programs themselves have also been criticized. For example, Alba and Lavin (1981) concluded that community college attendance worked to gradually dampen students' educational aspirations, regardless of academic performance. Critics have also charged that transfer education inadequately prepares students for four-year schools, which results in a lower baccalaureate attainment rate for students starting in two-year colleges compared with those who began at a four-year college. Indeed, there is evidence that if students are equally matched on variables of academic aptitude, race, ethnicity, gender, and so forth, those who start at a community college are at least 15 percent less likely to attain a bachelor's degree than those who start at a four-year school (Pascarella and Terenzini, 2005). What this perspective ignores, however, is that for some students, starting at a four-year college is not an option because of escalating tuition costs and students' family or job responsibilities. Because critics of the transfer function focus on transfer rates and transfer students' baccalaureate attainment, in this chapter we look at estimates of transfer rates and studies of the success of transfer students. We also examine current developments influencing transfer rates and the transfer mission and speculate about the future of this mission.

Transfer Rates and Transfer Student Performance

Although community colleges have faced much criticism for low transfer rates, no organization or state has ever issued an official statement about what an acceptable transfer rate would be (Townsend, 2002). Apparently, critics believe that if all students expressing an initial interest in transfer upon entering the community college do not do so, the institution has failed.

Transfer rates have fluctuated over time, but likely have never been above 33 percent. Current national estimates of transfer rates vary depending on the definition of transfer student. The Center for the Study of Community Colleges (2001) uses this definition: "All students entering the two-year college in a given year who have no prior college experience and who complete at least 12 college credit units [at that college] within four years, divided into the number of that group who take one or more classes at an in-state, public university within four years" (p. 1). According to this definition, the national rate of transfer ranged from 21.2 to 23.7 percent between 1984 and 1989, and was 25.18 percent in 1995 (Townsend, 2002). The National Effective Transfer Consortium, however, defines transfer rate as the number of people who transferred to a four-year school in the fall after having been at a community college the previous semester and having completed at least six credits (Berman, Curry, Nelson, and Weiler, 1990). Using this definition, transfer rates averaged 25 percent during the 1980s (Townsend, 2002).

These definitions concentrate on number of credit hours transferred, but ignore or exclude any consideration of the kinds of courses taken. For example, were students enrolled in transfer-level academic classes or terminal vocational education courses, which may or may not transfer to four-year institutions? This point is important because some comments about declining transfer rates include only students in transfer programs or recipients of the associate of arts degree (Townsend, 2002). Transfer rate calculations in which only associate of arts recipients are included ignore the reality that many students in vocationally oriented two-year programs have always transferred to four-year colleges and universities. For example, in Florida the associate of science degree is considered a terminal degree. Yet almost 6 percent of students who started in fall 1993 in associate of science programs in the Florida Community College System subsequently transferred to Florida's state university system (Florida Department of Education, 1999). In Washington, 10 percent of students with the associate of applied science degree, considered a terminal or nontransfer degree in that state, currently transfer to four-year institutions (Seppanen, 2005). Including these students in transfer calculations increases institutional, state, and national transfer rates. How well do students transfer?

In addition to long-standing concerns about the rate or percentage of community college students who transfer to four-year institutions, there have also been concerns about how well these students perform after transfer. Hence, there have been many studies of community college transfer students' academic performance. In one of the earliest such examinations, Koos (1925) compared the academic performance of ninety-five two-year college graduates who transferred to one of nineteen four-year institutions with seventy-five "native" students, who began postsecondary study at the University of Minnesota, where Koos was a faculty member. He concluded, *"There is no appreciable difference in the degrees of success in the work of the junior years of junior-college graduates and of those who do their first two years of work in a standard university"* (pp. 95–96, italics in the original).

More recent studies have examined grade point average (GPA) the first semester after transfer to look for evidence of transfer shock as manifested by a drop in GPA. Other researchers have examined declines in GPA over time or rates of baccalaureate attainment. Many studies also take students' individual characteristics into account to determine which are related to persistence and academic performance. These studies usually include ethnicity, gender, age, transfer credit hours, and transfer GPA, and find some variation in academic performance based on these individual variables. However, almost all studies find that community college transfer students do as well or almost as well as native students, although there is often an initial drop in performance during their first semester (Carlan and Byxbe, 2000; Glass and Harrington, 2002; Koker and Hendel, 2003).

Thus, research indicates that transfer students' academic performance is rarely problematic, at least for those transfers who earned an associate degree. However, students who transfer before earning the associate degree are on average less successful at the senior institution. In general, the more credit hours a student has when she transfers, the greater the likelihood of academic success and baccalaureate attainment (McCormick and Carroll, 1997). However, if only students with associate degrees are counted as transfer students, the national rate of transfer would be far lower than the approximately 25 percent reported by the Center for the Study of Community Colleges and the National Effective Transfer Consortium.

Current Developments Affecting Transfer Rates and the Transfer Mission

In the next decade several developments may affect community college transfer rates, however defined, as well as the overall transfer function. These developments include community college actions, institutional capacity issues, national activities, and individual student behaviors.

Community College Actions. To increase institutional transfer rates, individual community colleges are working to develop programs and relationships with specific four-year colleges to improve the transferability of students and courses. As Chapter Five in this volume describes, honors programs are one way to improve some students' chances of being accepted at prestigious senior institutions. Other efforts to increase the likelihood that specific courses will transfer include developing course-by-course articulation agreements with individual four-year institutions, and perhaps more importantly, developing institutional and state-level articulation agreements for certain associate degrees. Articulation of the associate of arts degree is most common, but in the past few years states and individual two- and four-year colleges have focused on developing articulation agreements for the associate of applied science (A.A.S.) degree because increasing numbers of A.A.S. students wish to transfer. A recent survey of state higher education officials found that "the majority of states had developed one or more pathways to promote occupational/technical program transfer" (Ignash and Owens, 2005, p. 1). Also, some four-year institutions have developed applied baccalaureates specifically designed to incorporate the associate of applied science degree. Articulation agreements for these degrees count technical courses taken at community colleges as courses for the major. Transfer students with associate of applied science degrees are required to take more courses in the major and enough general education courses to meet the state's or the four-year institution's general education requirements. For example, Northwest Missouri State University has an articulation agreement with Metropolitan Area Community Colleges for a bachelor of science in business. Under this articulation agreement, students who have an associate of applied science in general business can transfer up to 84 credits (encompassing the 63 credit hours needed for the associate of applied science and 21 additional hours in general education courses). Because the total hours needed for the baccalaureate is 124, the transfer students may only need to take 40 hours, or about eighteen months

NEW DIRECTIONS FOR COMMUNITY COLLEGES • DOI: 10.1002/cc

of courses at the senior institution (DeYoung, 2001). In other words, they can transfer credits equivalent to the first two and one-half years of college.

Other institutional efforts to increase the baccalaureate attainment of students starting at a community college include partnerships with four-year colleges and universities to offer courses that count toward the bachelor's degree on the community college campus. A more advanced version of this approach is developing a university center on a two-year college campus. In these partnerships, students are accepted into a university program and their credits are accepted toward the baccalaureate, yet they do not need to physically attend another institution. It is not clear whether states or institutions count these students as transfer students; including them might increase institutional and state transfer rates.

In 1994 Dougherty stated that the community college transfer mission should be tightly coupled to the four-year institution. Indeed, he believed that community colleges should be branches of the four-year school or even become senior institutions themselves. This thinking may be becoming a reality today, as selected community colleges in several states—including Florida, Texas, and Utah—have sought to increase the number of community college students attaining the baccalaureate by offering and awarding the degree themselves (Floyd and Skolnik, 2005). Dubbed the community college baccalaureate, or CCB, and defined as a baccalaureate awarded by the community college, this controversial degree may affect transfer rates in certain programs. Thus a community college offering a baccalaureate in programs offered at nearby four-year colleges would likely see a decline in transfer rates to those institutions. More specifically, students who might have transferred from a community college to a nearby four-year college's teacher education program may stay at the community college to attain a baccalaureate in teacher education (Townsend and Ignash, 2003). Under these circumstances, the rate of baccalaureate attainment for a state's citizens would not necessarily increase, but a particular institution's transfer rate would decline.

Institutional Capacity Issues. Several states are experiencing institutional capacity issues that affect the likelihood that a community college student is able to transfer to a four-year school. In 2003–04, California community colleges were unable to accommodate approximately 175,000 students; that same year, North Carolina's two-year institutions had to turn away over 50,000 students (Phillippe and Sullivan, 2005). Several of Florida's community colleges also had to turn away students because of limited capacity ("Enrollment Increasing, Many Students Turned Away," 2004). Similarly, four-year institutions in the state of Washington have had limited capacity for several years, making the acceptance of community college transfer students more problematic than in the past (Sausner, 2004; "UW Struggling to Accommodate All Transfer Students," 2005).

National Activities. Across the nation many organizations are working to increase baccalaureate attainment rates by facilitating articulation and transfer of credits. For example, the American Association of Community Colleges (2004) has detailed some important pretransfer problems as well as state and system barriers to transfer, such as financial aid policies. Similarly, the National Articulation and Transfer Network, funded by the Fund for the Improvement of Postsecondary Education and several foundations, is working to facilitate the transfer of courses across state lines. Recent congressional discussions that are part of the reauthorization of the Higher Education Act have also focused on the issue of transferability of courses and credits. Influenced by for-profit institutions seeking to have their institutions' credits accepted by nonprofit colleges, congressional members are becoming increasingly aware of the need for agreements that facilitate interinstitutional transfer and increase baccalaureate attainment.

Student Behaviors. Greater attention to the transferability of course credits is partially influenced by certain student behaviors. One such behavior is the increase in the percentage of A.A.S. recipients seeking to attain a baccalaureate, as already noted. Many high school students take dual enrollment courses, either at a community college or at their high schools. Dual enrollment courses are becoming increasingly popular because they provide an early and eased entry into college course work, strengthen the high school curriculum, increase postsecondary access for students traditionally underrepresented in higher education, act as a recruitment tool for colleges, and accelerate students' time to degree (Andrews, 2001). Over 70 percent of public high schools offered dual enrollment opportunities in 2002–03, primarily at community colleges (Waits, Setzer, and Lewis, 2005).

If students choose to matriculate at the college offering the dual enrollment course, they have gained a head start on their college degree. If they decide to attend a different college, they must try to transfer any dual credit courses to the college where they matriculate. Although high school students participating in community college dual enrollment classes are not classified as transfer students, they do transfer community college courses if they later attend four-year colleges. They also increase enrollment in two-year academic degree programs. Thus, offering dual enrollment courses can be considered an extension of the transfer mission.

Another student behavior affecting the transfer mission is the somewhat common practice of four-year college students attending community colleges concurrently or during the summer to shorten their time to baccalaureate degree completion. Adelman (2004) reports that 6 percent of all students in the high school class of 1992 used the community college in this way. However, because his analysis focused only on traditional-age students, it is likely that far more students engage in this practice, given the high percentage of non-traditional-age college students at community colleges. Like dual enrollment students, these four-year college students are not classified as transfer students, but they benefit greatly from the community college's transfer mission.

NEW DIRECTIONS FOR COMMUNITY COLLEGES • DOI: 10.1002/cc

Future of the Transfer Mission

What is the likely impact of the developments described in the preceding paragraphs on the community college's transfer mission? On the one hand, the importance of this mission would seem to be strengthened by greater interest in the transferability of community college courses. The mission is also supported by increasing enrollments of traditional-age students, many of whom will aspire to the baccalaureate. By 2012 over three million U.S. students will graduate from high school each year with a peak of 3.2 million in 2008–09 (Gerald and Hussar, 2002, as cited in Kimmel, 2005). This increase will affect community college enrollments: by 2012, undergraduate enrollment is projected to be over 17.5 million. According to Kimmel (2005), "enrollments at two-year public institutions are projected to grow by about 12 percent during the 2001–2012 period" (p. 35). Many of these enrollments will be in transfer programs. Institutional, state, and national efforts to develop articulation agreements for individual courses and degrees—especially in applied areas—also strengthen the visibility and viability of the transfer mission. These articulation efforts should also increase transfer rates, particularly among associate degree recipients.

A threat to the mission, at least in terms of institutional accountability for transfer rates, may be the growing movement among community colleges to award the baccalaureate themselves. It is too soon to tell if every state will grant individual community colleges the right to confer the baccalaureate, but currently at least twelve states have done so or are considering doing so. As indicated earlier, offering one or more CCB programs may have a negative effect on an institution's transfer rate, even though it may actually increase baccalaureate degree attainment. If an institution's transfer rates are lowered because it offers the CCB, will legislators, policy analysts, and scholars understand the connection or will they escalate criticism of the school's transfer rates, and by extension, community college transfer rates in general?

With the possible exception of the community college baccalaureate, recent developments suggest that the transfer mission is and will continue to be a key curricular mission of the comprehensive community college. However, until researchers and institutional leaders gain a better understanding of why some students' likelihood of attaining a baccalaureate is weakened by starting at a community college, there will be a significant number of students who wander off the transfer path and fail to achieve the baccalaureate. Community college leaders, faculty, policymakers, and researchers must focus on this group of students in order to strengthen the traditional community college transfer mission.

References

Adelman, C. *Principal Indicators of Student Academic Histories in Postsecondary Education, 1972–2000.* Washington, D.C.: U.S. Department of Education, 2004.

Alba, R. D., and Lavin, D. E. "Community Colleges and Tracking in Higher Education." *Sociology of Education,* 1981, *54,* 223–237.

American Association of Community Colleges. *Improving Access to the Baccalaureate.* Washington, D.C.: American Association of Community Colleges, 2004.

Andrews, H. A. *The Dual-Credit Phenomenon! Challenging Secondary School Students Across 50 States.* Stillwater, Okla.: New Forums Press, 2001.

Berman, P., Curry, J., Nelson, B., and Weiler, D. *Enhancing Transfer Effectiveness: A Model for the 1990s.* First-Year Report to the National Effective Transfer Consortium. Berkeley: BW Associates, 1990. (ED 324 050)

Carlan, P. E., and Byxbe, F. R. "Community Colleges Under the Microscope: An Analysis of Performance Predictors for Native and Transfer Students." *Community College Review,* 2000, *28*(2), 27–42.

Center for the Study of Community Colleges. *National Transfer Assembly Results: Update for 1995.* Los Angeles: University of California, Los Angeles, ERIC Clearinghouse for Community Colleges, 2001. http://www.gseis.ucla.edu/ccs/edinfos/edin0104.html. Accessed Aug. 17, 2006.

Cohen, A. M., and Brawer, F. B. *The American Community College.* (4th ed.) San Francisco: Jossey-Bass, 2003.

DeYoung, R. C. *Successful AAS-BS Partnerships: Models for Articulation.* Paper presented at the annual Missouri Transfer and Articulation Conference, Lake of the Woods, Mo., Feb. 2001.

Dougherty, K. J. *The Contradictory College: The Conflicting Origins, Impacts, and Futures of the Community College.* Albany: State University of New York Press, 1994.

"Enrollment Increasing, Many Students Turned Away." *Florida Community College Newsletter.* (No. 2002–010), Sept. 17, 2004, p. 1.

Florida Department of Education. *Outcomes: A Longitudinal Look at the Class of Fall 1993* (Data Trends 13). Tallahassee: Florida Department of Education, 1999. http://www.fldoe.org/CC/OSAS/DataTrendsResearch/DT-13.pdf. Accessed Aug. 17, 2006.

Floyd, D., and Skolnik, M. L. "Perspectives on the Community College Baccalaureate." In D. Floyd, M. L. Skolnik, and K. Walker (eds.), *The Community College Baccalaureate: Emerging Trends and Policy Issues.* Sterling, Va.: Stylus, 2005.

Glass, J. C., Jr., and Harrington, A. R. "Academic Performance of Community College Transfer Students and 'Native' Students at a Large State University." *Community College Journal of Research and Practice,* 2002, *26,* 415–430.

Ignash, J. M., and Owens, K. R. *Pathways and Portions of Pathways: How States are Articulating Occupational Programs.* Paper presented at the third Biennial Conference on Transfer and Articulation, Indianapolis, July 2005.

Karabel, J. "Community Colleges and Social Stratification." *Harvard Educational Review,* 1972, *42,* 543–558.

Kimmel, E. W. "Who Is at the Door? The Demography of Higher Education in the 21st Century." In W. J. Camara and E. W. Kimmel (eds.), *Choosing Students: Higher Education Admissions Tools for the 21st Century.* Hillsdale, N.J.: Erlbaum, 2005.

Koker, M., and Hendel, D. D. "Predicting Graduation Rates for Three Groups of New Advanced-Standing Cohorts." *Community College Journal of Research & Practice,* 2003, *27,* 131–146.

Koos, L. V. *The Junior-College Movement.* Westport, Conn: Greenwood Press, 1925.

McCormick, A. C., and Carroll, C. D. *Transfer Behavior Among Beginning Postsecondary Students, 1989–94.* Washington, D.C.: U.S. Department of Education, 1997.

Pascarella, E. T., and Terenzini, P. T. (eds.). *How College Affects Students.* Vol. 2. San Francisco: Jossey-Bass, 2005.

Phillippe, K., and Sullivan, L. G. *National Profile of Community Colleges: Trends & Statistics.* Washington, D.C.: American Association of Community Colleges, 2005.

Sausner, R. "Are We Shutting Her Out?" *University Business,* May 2004, 33–37. http://www.universitybusiness.com/page.cfm?p=525. Accessed Aug. 17, 2006.

Seppanen, L. "Federal and State Issues Relating to Transfer: Washington State." Paper presented at the third Biennial Conference on Transfer and Articulation, Indianapolis, July 2005.

Townsend, B. K. "Transfer Rates: A Problematic Criterion for Measuring the Community College." In T. H. Bers and H. D. Calhoun (eds.), *Next Steps for the Community College.* New Directions for Community Colleges, no. 117. San Francisco: Jossey-Bass, 2002.

Townsend, B. K., and Ignash, J. M. "Community College Roles in Teacher Education: Current Approaches and Future Possibilities." In B. K. Townsend and J. M. Ignash (eds.), *The Role of the Community College in Teacher Education.* New Directions for Community Colleges, no. 121. San Francisco: Jossey-Bass, 2003.

"UW Struggling to Accommodate All Transfer Students." *Community College Week,* July 18, 2005, p. 3.

Waits, T., Setzer, C. J., and Lewis, L. *Dual Credit and Exam-Based Courses in U.S. Public High Schools: 2002–2003* (NCES 2005–009). Washington, D.C.: U. S. Department of Education, National Center for Education Statistics, 2005.

Zwerling, S. *Second Best: The Crisis of the Community College.* New York: McGraw-Hill, 1976.

BARBARA K. TOWNSEND *is professor of higher and continuing education at the University of Missouri-Columbia and a former community college faculty member and administrator.*

KRISTIN B. WILSON *is professor of English at Moberly Area Community College in Missouri.*

NEW DIRECTIONS FOR COMMUNITY COLLEGES • DOI: 10.1002/cc

5

*This chapter describes community college honors pro-
grams and courses, emphasizing in particular the Honors
College at Miami Dade College in Florida. The chapter
discusses pros and cons of honors programs and courses
in the context of their appropriateness to the community
college mission of open access and egalitarianism.*

Prioritizing Service to the Academically Talented: The Honors College

Deborah L. Floyd, Alexandria Holloway

Historically, community colleges have emphasized their societal missions of
egalitarianism and open access as integral curricular components. As open
admissions colleges, these institutions have been challenged to prepare a
wide variety of students with an equally wide variety of reasons for
enrolling. Because they are place-bound or have limited finances, some students may choose a community college for their first two years of the baccalaureate. Others who are academically underprepared for college opt to
complete developmental classes at the community college, hoping to transfer to a university after finishing such studies. Many more students choose
the community college as an avenue to prepare for the world of work
through workforce and technical training. Over time, however, community
colleges have expanded their curricular foci to include other priorities. One
such priority is programming for the academically gifted and ambitious.
Through the functional mission of offering honors courses and programs,
the community college addresses its societal mission of egalitarianism by
ensuring that all people have equal access to educational opportunities at
all academic levels.

Honors programs first appeared in community colleges in the 1950s
and 1960s (Barnes and Woodward, 1959; Bogdan, 1962; Bradshaw, 1962).
These early efforts were usually accelerated courses offered to academically
talented students who had expressed interest in specific areas of study. Since
that time, community college honors programs have gained considerable

New Directions for Community Colleges, no. 136, Winter 2006 © 2006 Wiley Periodicals, Inc.
Published online in Wiley InterScience (www.interscience.wiley.com) • DOI: 10.1002/cc.258

strength. In the 1980s community colleges shifted their emphasis from merely open access and egalitarianism to academic quality, especially related to transfer courses (Byrne, 1998). Today, "about half of two-year colleges now support honors programs—an increase of almost 50 percent over the last decade" (Beck, 2003, p. 5).

This movement has created discussion among community college advocates and critics alike. A powerful argument for honors programs is that they enhance the community college mission by providing qualified students with open access to superior academic courses and programming. Because many academically talented students are place-bound or have other obligations that prevent them from beginning at a four-year university, advocates of honors programs argue that they should be afforded the same opportunities for honors courses and programs that are an accepted part of university curricula. Indeed, they contend that community college honors programs enrich the academic curriculum and may actually enhance a student's ability to transfer to elite baccalaureate-granting institutions. Thus, advocates argue, honors programs are congruent with the equalitarian focus of the community college mission (Outcalt, 1999).

Critics counter, however, that most community college honors programs employ selective admissions criteria; not everyone has equal access to these programs. Furthermore, as Kisker and Outcalt (2005) point out, many critics believe that honors programs "introduce a note of elitism into the egalitarian goals of community colleges" (p. 3). These critics assert that such selective programming has no place in an open access community college. Furthermore, as Wattenbarger cautions, "would-be honors students could fall victim to sometimes overinflated claims made by community college honors programs" (Beck, 2003, p. 5). In fact, another criticism of community college honors programming is that although there are numerous articles describing the programs, there is little research documenting their outcomes (Bulakowski and Townsend, 1995; Kisker and Outcalt, 2005).

This chapter describes community college honors programs and highlights several models, especially the efforts of Miami Dade College. Pros and cons of honors programs in community colleges are discussed in the context of their appropriateness to the institution's mission of providing egalitarian access to academic opportunities at all levels.

Honors Programs: Forms and Models

Admission into community college honors programs can be classified into two forms—honors courses open to all students regardless of academic preparation, and restricted enrollment courses for students who meet certain academic requirements (Burnett, 2005). As an example of the first form, North Harris Community College in Texas invites any student to enroll in honors courses. According to the program director, this open enrollment policy is attractive to students who may have struggled in high school but

NEW DIRECTIONS FOR COMMUNITY COLLEGES • DOI: 10.1002/cc

who have the potential to succeed in college-level academic work. In contrast, the College of Lake County in Illinois restricts admission to students with a high school or college grade point average (GPA) of 3.5, a minimum of twelve credit hours, and a recommendation from an advisory committee.

Although these two colleges illustrate different honors admissions philosophies, both share the perspective that these programs are appropriately included in their college's overall mission and enhance students' academic experiences. What is important to recognize here is that both these institutions manifest the *mission* of the community college by offering *programmatic* honors opportunities. In both examples, the honors program does not exist as ancillary to the college, but rather is an integral curricular offering that provides yet another group of students with a rich learning experience.

Community college honors programs are offered in several formats. Many community colleges add to standard courses by including more academically rigorous content and additional requirements such as labs, special research projects, or experiential activities to enhance students' creative abilities. To illustrate, Michigan's Henry Ford Community College (HFCC) offers an honors program that includes core courses in English composition, science, and the humanities. This program also emphasizes library research, computer databases, and Internet research. The HFCC program is structured around several core courses but is flexible enough to fit almost any major field of study (Henry Ford Community College, 2006).

Some colleges, like Florida's Hillsborough Community College (HCC), have created honors institutes or departments. In addition to offering over forty honors courses, the HCC Honors Institute offers students three forms of honors distinction: graduation from the Honors Institute if they complete a minimum of eight honors courses (twenty-four credit hours); graduation with an Honors Certificate if they do not fulfill all Honors Institute requirements but complete at least twelve hours of honors classwork with an overall GPA of at least 3.0; and graduation with Distinction in Honors if they complete the Honors Institute with a minimum overall GPA of at least 3.0 (Hillsborough Community College, 2004). Honors students also receive priority registration privileges and opportunities to participate in field trips, study abroad programs, and specialized leadership activities.

Valencia Community College (VCC), also in Florida, offers an honors program for some one thousand students on four campuses. The program attracts a large number of valedictorians and salutatorians from local feeder high schools, as well as students from surrounding states and foreign countries. Almost half of these students receive full tuition scholarships; approximately two-thirds receive full tuition scholarships when they transfer to four-year colleges and universities, although not all of the university scholarships are formally linked to successful completion of the VCC honors program.

Santa Monica College (California) offers each term a Scholars Program to four hundred students who want to take courses focusing on "mastery of subject matter demonstrated through writing, research, critical thinking, and analysis" (Santa Monica College, n.d., n.p.). This program focuses on designated sections of general education classes and sets class enrollments at twenty-five students. Students may graduate from the honors program after completing fifteen units in the Scholars Program with an overall GPA of at least 3.0. Partially as a result of its Scholars Program, Santa Monica College boasts that it is "number one in transfers" for the past fifteen years to the University of California system. Scholars Program students receive priority admissions consideration to University of California, Los Angeles, and several other universities, along with special counseling, workshops, priority registration, smaller class sizes, and special college tours.

Established in 1968, the Honors Program at Rockland Community College (RCC) in New York was designed to challenge students by strengthening the curriculum in the liberal arts and sciences. The RCC Honors Program boasts a rich history of personalized and intellectually stimulating offerings for students who desire to participate in a few honors classes, as well as those electing to complete specific honors courses as an honors concentration. Two curricular tracks are offered: the Mentor-Talents Students track for students in the arts and sciences, and a Management Development track for business, management, finance, marketing, or programming students. Nearly 100 percent of RCC's Honors Program graduates have maintained a 3.0 average at four-year colleges (Rockland Community College, n.d.).

Students have two ways of participating in honors programs at the College of DuPage in Illinois. They may elect to enroll in individual honors courses, or they can participate in the Honors Scholars Program. Each quarter, the College of DuPage enrolls hundreds of students in honors courses; the Honors Scholar Program currently has over seven hundred members. The college boasts that 100 percent of its students completing the Honors Scholars Program have successfully transferred to universities, and one participant has become a Rhodes Scholar (College of DuPage, 2006).

Prince George's Community College (PGCC) was the first Maryland community college to establish an honors academy and honors program. The PGCC Honors Academy program is a selective admissions program. In addition to honors classes, students are expected to perform at least fifteen hours of community service work each semester. PGCC also has a number of articulation agreements with private and public universities and colleges to ensure successful transfer of its honors courses. In 2002, PGCC and St. Mary's College announced a dual admissions program for Honors Academy students; both institutions provide financial assistance for students, scholarships, and other support (Prince George's Community College, 2002).

Other programmatic features of community college honors programs include opportunities for cultural, community, and civic engagement. For example, the Honors Program at San Jacinto College (Texas) includes opportunities for students to make presentations at national, state, and local conferences, and to publish papers in a regional honors journal (San Jacinto College, 2006).

NEW DIRECTIONS FOR COMMUNITY COLLEGES • DOI: 10.1002/cc

The Honors College at Miami Dade College

Miami Dade College (MDC) in Florida has one of the most notable Honors College programs in the United States. Before 2001, each MDC campus had its own honors program; each program operated independently and did not share curricula or evaluation criteria. To better meet the needs of gifted students, to provide constancy among campuses in eligibility and maintenance requirements, and to offer a progressive curriculum with meaningful service and enrichment opportunities, MDC's president envisioned a unified, stand-alone honors program. Thus, the former separate campus programs were dissolved with the understanding that currently enrolled students would continue to receive their benefits until they completed their program. In 2001, the Honors College at MDC was created as a separate college in the greater Miami Dade College District, and an inaugural class of 75 students was admitted in fall 2002. This first class was housed on the Wolfson Campus; in fall 2003, the Honors College expanded to include 75 new students at each of the Wolfson, North, and Kendall campuses. This expansion allowed for greater accessibility to honors classes for students throughout the entire county. In fall 2004 the Honors College enrolled a total of 365 students.

The MDC Honors College is designed to meet the needs of a select group of goal-oriented, academically talented students. The Honors College curriculum provides a gamut of rich collegiate experiences for students, and includes both academic and support services. It is important to note that the MDC Honors College has been supported and promoted by MDC leadership and is considered one of the district's priorities. The MDC Honors College prides itself on adhering to the standards set by the National Collegiate Honors Council and being "fully institutionalized so as to build thereby a genuine tradition of excellence" (Miami Dade College, 2004, p. 1).

Several distinguishing factors characterize Miami Dade Honors College. First, the program has been endorsed by the administration, supported by the faculty and staff, and widely accepted by enrolled students. Second, the program has been phased in slowly to accommodate a variety of approaches over time. Third, the program includes both academic and student support services. A generous financial aid package, collegewide support services, and enrichment activities including attendance and participation at national and regional conferences, internships, mentoring assignments with corporate coaches, study travel tours, university transfer counseling, a personalized educational plan with seamless registration, and an individual Honors College e-mail address are just a few of the resources available to MDC honors students (Miami Dade College, 2004). All students admitted into the Honors College receive the Honors College Fellows Scholarship Award, which includes the equivalent of in-state tuition, a book allowance, and a stipend. The award is renewable for each term as long as the student is in good standing and maintains a 3.5 GPA.

NEW DIRECTIONS FOR COMMUNITY COLLEGES • DOI: 10.1002/cc

Honors Students. The majority of MCC's honors students are Hispanic (73 percent), followed by black (14 percent), white (10 percent), and Asian (3 percent). Sixty-eight percent are female. Students are more traditional in age: the average student age is nineteen, although students range in age from seventeen to forty-eight. Approximately 96 percent of the honors students who were first-time college students enrolled at MDC immediately after high school graduation. Since Miami Dade College serves an ethnically diverse student clientele, it is not surprising that Spanish is the native language of almost half of the students (49 percent), with students speaking over eighteen different languages. More than half are U.S. citizens (63 percent); the remaining are from twenty-six different countries (Cuba, Colombia, and Venezuela are the most common).

Most honors students graduated from thirty-six of Miami Dade County's public high schools and nine of its private high schools; the remainder graduated from out-of-county schools or were home-schooled. The average high school GPA of admitted students was 4.17, and the average SAT score was 1273 in 2004 (up from 4.16 and 1271 in 2003). Honors students majored in forty different programs, with pre–bachelor of arts, biology, and business administration most frequently chosen.

These demographics reflect the larger community served by the college. Critics who believe that honors programs are not egalitarian should note that Miami Dade's program serves a diverse clientele of students. Furthermore, the high levels of minority and female participation suggest that this program is truly geared to all students.

Honors College Program Elements and Outcomes. Miami Dade's Honors College has provided a rich array of experiences for both students and faculty. Students are required to attend biweekly colloquia featuring guest speakers and faculty presentations, have opportunities to participate in study travel events such as the Salzburg Seminars, Washington Center Seminars, Business and Dining Etiquette Seminars, and innumerable cultural and social activities.

The rigorous courses provide students with a high degree of faculty interaction and multiple opportunities to engage in learning communities formed by discipline interests. Important aspects of the curriculum include the development of leadership skills and the assessment of ethical and civic responsibilities. To graduate from the Honors College, students must retain a 3.5 GPA, complete six credits in leadership courses and twenty hours of service per term, and earn a minimum of thirty-six credits in honors-designated courses.

The retention rate for students participating in the Honors College is 88 percent. In addition, nearly all honors students have been admitted into their first-choice university, including such institutions as Yale, Columbia, Georgia Tech, Washington University, Amherst, Cornell, Georgetown, Mount Holyoke, Northwestern, the University of Chicago, New York University, Barnard, Smith, and the University of Wisconsin. Graduates whose first choice is Florida International University (FIU) receive a generous full tuition scholarship and are admitted into FIU's Honors College. MDC holds similar agreements with the University of Miami and Florida Atlantic University (Miami Dade College, 2004). Moreover, administrative support and the integration of the program into the fabric of the college have clearly established this endeavor as one of the college's priorities. Indeed, faculty and student interactions that have resulted from the program have helped create an engaging scholarly community that enhances students' self-esteem and encourages them to break out of their comfort zone and seek knowledge and their place in the world.

Individual Honors Courses. Initially designed to meet the needs of a select group of goal-oriented, academically talented students who could endure more strenuous intellectual examination, benefit from more faculty-student interaction, and thrive in a highly focused, multidimensional learning environment, the Honors College has entered into yet another phase. Recently, MDC began offering independent, stand-alone honors courses for students who want to challenge themselves and earn honors credits for graduation but who cannot enroll in a full program of study. These courses are especially important for the many Miami Dade students who work full-time. The college anticipates that these individual honors courses will allow even more students to benefit from a challenging and intensive academic experience, as well as productive interactions with other students who share a similar passion for learning (Miami Dade College, 2004).

Are Honors Programs Appropriate for All Community Colleges?

Critics have argued that honors colleges are not appropriate for all community colleges, given differing sizes, missions, and foci. Indeed, some commonalities exist among community colleges offering honors programs—at least those reviewed in this chapter. Most of the colleges are larger institutions with five thousand or more students, offer a variety of curricular programs, and are located in or near major metropolitan areas. One might surmise, then, that a larger student body and more diverse curricular offerings are required for the successful operation of an honors program. Another important feature common to the honors programs described in this chapter is the strong support of senior administration and staff. This support and the acknowledgment that an honors program is central to the mission of the college seem to provide stability for its development and sustainability. Moreover, all of the colleges discussed in this chapter have a committed and trained faculty willing to develop curricula and provide academic support for students. Finally, one cannot deny the importance of the students who participate in honors programs. Whether measured through retention rates or successful transfer to senior institutions, students who have positive experiences in honors programs become the best advertisers.

Table 5.1. Honors Colleges: Pros and Cons

Issue	Pros	Cons
Mission: Access	Honors colleges extend commitment to equal access to academically rigorous programs, especially for place-bound, minority, and underserved populations—an extension of egalitarianism.	Honors programs detract from commitment to other key curricular priorities; they are one step toward elitism.
Baccalaureate degrees and transfer: Access	Honors programs promote greater access to baccalaureate degrees, including scholarships for honors students to prestigious universities and colleges. They may enhance transfer success.	Honors colleges may discourage gifted students from attending prestigious universities as freshmen.
Community college size: Access	Honors colleges tend to be located at larger community colleges with greater capacity to deliver comprehensive offerings.	Honors programs may not be found in smaller community colleges with limited capacity to offer such courses and programs.
Classes	Honors classes are often smaller, so students receive more personalized attention.	Classes are often limited to honors students (or have selective enrollments), thus segregating students from more typical community college students.
Curriculum	Honors curricula consist of a variety of stimulating learning experiences for students.	There should be similar experiences and challenges for students in regular courses as for those in honors programs.
Faculty	Honors programs have trained and certified faculty who provide a high level of academic leadership for honors students.	Honors colleges may create faculty hierarchies. For example, faculty who teach gifted students may be more highly rewarded than those who teach regular or developmental students.
Nonacademic factors	Honors colleges can enhance students' self-esteem.	Honors programs may cause students to expect similar nurturing at four-year institutions.

Can honors programs be successfully implemented at smaller community colleges with less curricular diversity? Absolutely. Most—if not all—of the programs described in this chapter started as small programs with limited courses. In fact, smaller community colleges may have an advantage over larger community colleges because faculty-student relationships are more likely to be personalized on smaller campuses. Furthermore, honors programs are not just limited to liberal arts majors, but embrace students in business, sciences, management, and other fields.

Pros and Cons of Community College Honors Programs

Whether one is an advocate or a critic of community college honors programs, there are several pros and cons of such programs. These are summarized in Table 5.1. The table is by no means an exhaustive list; rather, it summarizes some of the controversial issues surrounding community college honors programs.

Conclusion

The larger question of whether honors programs are congruent with the open access and egalitarianism mission of community colleges is, perhaps, only a matter of rhetoric. After all, the community college's societal mission to be responsive to its local community requires institutions to offer curricular programming to meet emerging needs and wants. When community college students needed developmental education courses to succeed in college-level work, community colleges changed their curricula to add these classes. Likewise, when increasing numbers of community college students aspired to the baccalaureate and asked for a rigorous curricula to prepare them for prestigious universities, community colleges changed their curricula to address those needs and wants. Like developmental courses that serve as bridges between secondary and postsecondary institutions, honors courses can be stepping-stones to four-year colleges and universities (Kisker and Outcalt, 2005); both curricular adaptations are key examples of responsive programming that meet emerging student wants and needs. Like developmental education and other key areas of the community college curriculum, honors courses and programs are well within the community college's mission of providing open access and opportunity to all students.

References

Barnes, C. M., and Woodward, D. H. "The Honors Program at Pratt Junior College." *Junior College Journal*, 1959, *30*(2), 77–78.
Beck, E. "It's an Honor." *Community College Week,* 2003, *15*, 4–6.
Bogdan, J. A. "Honors in History: A Junior College Experiment." *Junior College Journal*, 1962, *33*(4), 185–189.
Bradshaw, L. J. "A Science Honors Program for the Junior College." *Junior College Journal*, 1962, *32*(5), 284–287.

Bulakowski, D., and Townsend, B. K. "Evaluation of a Community College Honors Program: Problems and Possibilities." *Community College Journal of Research and Practice,* 1995, *19*(6), 485–499.

Byrne, J. P. "Honors Programs in Community Colleges: A Review of Recent Issues and Literature." *Community College Review,* 1998, *26*(2), 67–80.

Burnett, S. "Honors Programs Spark Controversy." *Community College Week,* 2005, *45,* n.p.

College of DuPage. "Honors: Getting Started." Glen Ellyn, Ill.: College of DuPage, 2006. http:www.cod.edu/Academic/AcadProg/Hon_Prog/Getting_started.htm. Accessed Aug. 17, 2006.

Henry Ford Community College. "Henry Ford II Honors Program." Dearborn, Mich.: Henry Ford Community College, 2006. http://www.hfcc.edu/about_us/honors_program.asp. Accessed Aug. 17, 2006.

Hillsborough Community College. *Hillsborough Community College Catalog 2004–2005.* Tampa, Fla.: Hillsborough Community College, 2004.

Kisker, C. B., and Outcalt, C. L. "Community College Honors and Developmental Faculty: Characteristics, Practices, and Implications for Access and Educational Equity." *Community College Review,* 2005, *33*(2), 1–21.

Miami Dade College. *Annual Report 2003–2004: The Honors College.* Miami: Miami Dade College, 2004.

Outcalt, C. "The Importance of Community College Honors Programs: An Overview." In G. Schuyler (ed.), *Trends in the Community College Curriculum.* New Directions for Community Colleges, no. 108. San Francisco: Jossey-Bass, 1999.

Prince George's Community College. *Community College Honors Academy and Maryland's Public Honors College Create Dual-Admission Program* (PGCC Press Release). Largo, Md.: Prince George's Community College, Apr. 26, 2002. http://www.pgcc.edu/pgweb/pgdocs/mpr/press_releases/2002/04/26/St_Marys_College_Honors_Signing.htm. Accessed Aug. 17, 2006.

Rockland Community College. "Nationally Renowned Honors Program: A Brilliant Start." Suffern, N.Y.: Rockland Community College, n.d. http://www.sunyrockland.edu/honors.html. Accessed Aug. 17, 2006.

San Jacinto College. "Honors Program." Pasadena, Tex.: San Jacinto College, 2006. http://www.sjcd.edu/future_students_courses_programs_honors.html. Accessed Aug. 17, 2006.

Santa Monica College. "Scholars Program." Santa Monica, Calif.: Santa Monica College, n.d. http://www.smc.edu/scholars/program.htm. Accessed Aug. 17, 2006.

DEBORAH L. FLOYD is professor and program leader of higher education leadership at Florida Atlantic University in Boca Raton. She has also been a community college president, vice president, and dean.

ALEXANDRIA HOLLOWAY is dean of the Honors College and professor of music at Miami Dade College in Florida.

NEW DIRECTIONS FOR COMMUNITY COLLEGES • DOI: 10.1002/cc

This chapter describes the evolution of the workforce development mission and its current crisis in the face of changing training demands, shriveling government support, and rising competition. Two alternative future paths are outlined: a baccalaureate degree-oriented new vocationalism and a renewed emphasis on serving the training needs of low-income adults.

The Uncertain Future of the Community College Workforce Development Mission

James Jacobs, Kevin J. Dougherty

One of the most significant contributions of community colleges to American higher education is their workforce preparation activity. Taken broadly, the community college workforce development mission includes all the institutional programs, courses, and activities that prepare students for work. This major institutional function cuts across specific organizational units, and is present in credit and noncredit programs, career and technical areas, and contract training units.

Roughly three-fifths of the over six million students in community college credit programs are pursuing some occupational course of study. In addition, millions of other Americans look to the community college for noncredit continuing education and job training. Community colleges have become a significant factor in local workforce development by taking advantage of institutional strengths such as organizational flexibility, close proximity to private-sector enterprises, low cost, technical expertise, and experience in teaching adult learners. Indeed, several states have built their incumbent worker training and business expansion programs around the community college (Dougherty and Bakia, 2000; Grubb and others, 1997).

Although policymakers and the public see workforce development as a fundamental mission of community colleges, it faces an extremely uncertain future because of structural changes in the economy and the emergence of new competitors. These developments have produced a quiet crisis in workforce development, and have resulted in divergent proposals for what

directions it should take. Currently, two somewhat contradictory positions are being advocated. On the one hand, proponents of a *new vocationalism* argue that community colleges should prepare individuals for high-tech jobs in computer technologies, teaching, and health care. In this view, community colleges should be gatekeepers for the skilled jobs of the future and a primary source of advanced technical training (Bragg, 2001). On the other hand, some advocate a renewed focus on meeting the needs of low-income workers: inner-city residents, new immigrants, and those displaced from traditional middle-class jobs because their manufacturing plants have closed. This perspective views the community college as an institution that can lift such people out of poverty by providing both basic education and occupational training (Grubb, Badway, and Bell, 2003; Matus-Grossman and Gooden, 2002; Prince and Jenkins, 2005). This chapter explores the evolution of the workforce development role of the community college, its interactions with other missions of the college, and the current crisis facing workforce development. In doing so, it will address the prospects for the new vocationalism versus low-income worker scenarios.

Evolution of Workforce Development

Occupational education arose soon after the formation of the first community colleges, but did not become a major community college mission until the 1950s and 1960s. During this period, governors, state legislators, and community college administrators strongly pushed for the vocationalization of community colleges in order to provide colleges with a distinct training niche and to stimulate the growth of state economies by offering publicly subsidized employee training in order to attract business firms (Brint and Karabel, 1989; Dougherty, 1994). In the early 1980s, when the post–Cold War U.S. economy began to unravel, community colleges moved into the center of efforts to revive the economic conditions of their local communities. Business firms were seeking to outsource their training as a way to cut costs, and state governments were willing to subsidize that outsourced training in hopes of retaining or attracting business investment. Meanwhile, community colleges saw contract training as a means of accruing enrollments, revenues, political ties, and curricular improvements (Dougherty and Bakia, 2000; Grubb and others, 1997). Much of this work was performed through noncredit instructional units that were often separate from traditional for-credit academic and occupational instruction.

By the end of the 1990s, workforce development units had become multimission centers with large nonacademic staffs and large numbers of students enrolled in noncredit occupational programs. According to the National Household Educational Survey, the noncredit student head count in public two-year colleges in 1995 was equivalent to about 90 percent of the for-credit head count. By 1999, noncredit enrollments exceeded credit enrollments by more than 8 percent (Government Accounting Office, 2005).

NEW DIRECTIONS FOR COMMUNITY COLLEGES • DOI: 10.1002/cc

As the community college workforce development function has expanded and changed, there have been repercussions, positive and negative, for other parts of the institution. Positively, the expansion and transformation of the workforce development mission allowed for a significant expansion and diversification of the community college. It also brought in many students, particularly those from less-advantaged backgrounds, who might never have otherwise attended—or been able to attend—the community college. Workforce development also generated new sources of revenue and helped create stronger connections with employers and state governments, which allowed community colleges to make up for stagnating state appropriations and counterbalance the power and prestige of four-year institutions. Finally, the expansion of contract training allowed colleges to revamp old-fashioned vocational programs by bringing in new information on what skills the labor market was demanding (Dougherty and Bakia, 2000; Grubb and others, 1997).

But there have also been negative repercussions of the expanded workforce development mission. Any time a part of an organization undergoes massive increases in activity, other parts may see their organizational prominence and access to resources decline. This certainly occurred as workforce education programs gained prominence. Faculty and staff in traditional academic areas of the college are often resentful of the attention workforce development attracts and fear that it will bring a change in the institution's values (Dougherty and Bakia, 2000). As well, the fact that fewer standards have been imposed on workforce courses reinforces perceptions that noncredit offerings are less rigorous than credit courses, which are commonly thought to constitute the core mission of the institution. In other words, despite their prevalence and popularity in community colleges, noncredit workforce development courses remain at the margins of the community college curriculum because they operate under different standards and structures (Grubb and others, 1997; Jacobs and Teahen, 1996).

Tensions also abound because the growth of workforce education may undercut the transfer function of the community college. As this mission has grown, it has pulled into terminal subbaccalaureate programs students who might otherwise have pursued a baccalaureate degree (Dougherty, 1994). In recent years, the transfer of occupational credits to four-year institutions has become easier, but students in occupational majors still have lower transfer rates than those in academic concentrations (Dougherty and Kienzl, 2006). Finally, the growth of occupational education has complicated the general education task of the community college. More specifically, occupational educators often demonstrate some resistance to general education, because they feel it takes away time from necessary technical instruction.

Despite these tensions, the American Association of Community Colleges (2000), after months of discussion and debate, delivered a ringing endorsement of the workforce development function: "Community colleges should view the preparation and development of the nation's workforce as a primary part of their mission and communicate to policymakers the uniqueness of this community college role" (p. 8). Yet despite this support, many argue that the community college workforce development mission is in crisis.

The Current Crisis in the Workforce Development Function

Three factors have contributed to the crisis in the community college's workforce development function: corporate demand for customized training has shriveled, state support has declined, and new competitors have appeared.

Changes in Employer Demand. The jobless recovery Americans have experienced since 2001 has weakened the demand for workforce training in three different ways. First, the training market for frontline hourly employees has shriveled as the number of these jobs continues to decline in the United States. Many of the largest customized training programs in the 1990s were in industries such as auto, steel, and aerospace that were modernizing to deal with international competition. Today, many of these firms have closed operations in the United States, and even when they have expanded their facilities, they hire workers with higher levels of education. As a result, firms are spending less on large-scale mass training programs and more on white-collar and technical training (Carnevale and Fry, 2002; Jacobs, 2001).

Second, there has been tremendous pressure on manufacturers to cut costs; this has influenced the amount of training being offered to workers. Companies are increasingly taking the stance that continuous skill upgrading and training is something individual workers need to pursue; it is no longer the company's responsibility (Bartlett, 2002). Third, along with the growing perception that training is an individual responsibility, employers are increasingly demanding degrees—especially bachelor's degrees—as opposed to workplace or technical skills. Employers perceive the college degree as a signal of a worker's motivation to complete an important milestone and as a marker of that person's capacity to benefit from additional training on the job. These three trends mean that although individual workers may attend the community college to earn an occupational degree or upgrade their skills, fewer and fewer employers are systematically using the institution as a training site.

Changes in State Support. Compounding the decline in business demand for workforce training is a weakening of state financial support for large-scale worker training programs. Many states still subsidize corporate training to lure new industry into their communities, but there has been a decrease in state economic development programs that target specific companies or sectors. Increasingly, many states have dropped ongoing general training programs in favor of onetime training targeted at obtaining new investments in the state (National Governors Association, 2005).

Even in states where there has been considerable industrial economic growth, workforce development programs differ considerably from those in the past. For example, in order to obtain large investments from Japanese and German auto manufacturers, southern states such as Alabama and Mississippi have required prospective workers to obtain training at their own expense in order to be eligible to work for the company. State training monies are spent primarily on training managers and white-collar workers, often at four-year colleges (Rosenfeld, Jacobs, and Liston, 2004).

At the federal level, the Workforce Investment Act (WIA) and Temporary Assistance for Needy Families (TANF) promote a work-first approach to handling clients and jobs that has also undercut community college workforce training programs. Training is deemphasized in favor of immediate job placement, which results in many workers finding work at insufficient incomes (Shaw and Goldrick-Rab, 2003). In addition, total funding devoted to WIA fell from a high of almost $5 billion to a little over $3.5 billion between 1998 and 2001. During that period, the number of individuals trained under WIA decreased from 168,000 to 72,000 (Spence and Kiel, 2003). The work-first mentality has made it less likely that businesses will rely on long-term community college programs for education and training (Matus-Grossman and Gooden, 2002; Shaw and Goldrick-Rab, 2003).

Instead, states have worked to increase the number of workers earning college degrees, particularly baccalaureates. The rationale is that a greater number of college graduates will give a state's economy a competitive edge in attracting high-tech businesses. Several states have assembled coalitions of public universities and community colleges to emphasize policies promoting dual enrollment between high schools and colleges, seamless transitions from community to four-year colleges and universities, and improved adult degree completion. Although community colleges certainly play a role in these strategies, the primary emphasis is on preparing students for the baccalaureate, rather than specific technical education (Austin, 2005).

Rise of New Competitors. Along with shriveling demand for worker training and declining state support, community colleges face challenges on the supply side. Beginning in the 1990s, many for-profit institutions developed customized degree programs directed at adults in large companies in order to take advantage of company tuition benefits. Unlike community colleges, private institutions such as the University of Phoenix and DeVry Institute of Technology tend to offer highly focused credit programs that are particularly successful in helping minority students earn technical degrees. In addition, there has been a significant growth of small for-profit trade schools aimed at working adults. Many of these trade schools are directed at frontline service and technology jobs, and take advantage of student loans to underwrite their activities. They advertise and market widely among low-income people who doubt they could ever attend college (Bailey, Badway, and Gumport, 2001; Deil-Amen and Rosenbaum, 2003).

Symbolic of the challenges facing the community college workforce development mission is the current state of nursing education. Community colleges produce over 65 percent of all nurses. Traditionally, associate degree in nursing programs attract adult students, particularly female heads of household. These programs are rigorous, full-time, and often take three years to complete. They have a clear curricular pathway that, if followed, will help students pass the licensure examination and obtain a job with a sustainable wage (Karp, Jacobs, and Hughes, 2002). However, many community college nursing programs are having difficulty attracting students with the necessary knowledge of mathematics, science, and other skills necessary to complete the programs. Furthermore, community college nursing programs are faced with intense competition from four-year bachelor's of science in nursing programs. Indeed, in large urban areas, the associate degree in nursing is losing some of its economic value in comparison to the bachelor's of science in nursing. If a strong program such as nursing is suffering this fate, what will be the future of other community college occupational programs such as computer networking, accounting, and education?

Conflicting Paths Toward the Future

Community college reactions to workforce development challenges described in the preceding paragraphs have been diverse and often contradictory. The primary choice has been between a new-vocationalism strategy that responds to the perceived needs of the business sector and a low-income worker strategy that focuses on lifting low-income workers out of poverty. The two approaches are not mutually exclusive, yet it is difficult to see how even the most comprehensive community college would be able to effectively implement both. Both strategies require reorientation and major institutional commitment of resources, which will be hard, given the increasing difficulties colleges face in raising revenues either from tuition or state appropriations.

The New Vocationalism. The concept behind this strategy is to prepare students for further education in the field rather than for an entry-level job. The federal prototype of this strategy is the decade-old Advanced Technology Education program of the National Science Foundation (NSF). This initiative—which consciously distances itself from traditional occupational education—stresses mathematics and science preparation for the emerging technologies of the future. Over three hundred different NSF projects are currently active in community colleges, and this program has likely stimulated the bulk of new curriculum development in the field of occupational education (Teles, 2005).

Furthermore, the new Community College Transitions Initiative (CCTI)—part of the federal redesign of the Perkins program—attempts to build community college and high school ties along specific career pathways. In contrast to Tech Prep programs, the CCTI initiative targets high school students who want to go on to the four-year college and are developing their foundation skills in high school (Hughes, 2006). Finally, the proliferation of information technology programs (IT) fits in the new vocationalism strategy. Though the IT boom of the late 1990s is over, over 90 percent of community colleges have developed programs in information technology. Originally these were based around industry certifications, but increasingly they have developed into programs that are linked to four-year degrees (Jacobs and Grubb, 2006).

For community college leaders, the new vocationalism strategy has many benefits. It permits colleges to attract better-prepared high school students. It also reinforces to state governors and legislators the significance of community colleges. But the strategy also faces obstacles. First, many university and community college faculty have not been interested in fostering occupational students' transfer to four-year institutions. However, states are making greater efforts to improve the transferability of occupational degrees by developing articulation agreements for occupational majors (Dougherty, Reid, and Nienhusser, 2006; Ignash and Kotun, 2005). Second, although new vocational programs are, in theory, open to all students, the basic skills needed for high-technology jobs are generally greater than those possessed by the average community college student. For example, a biotechnology technician training program in a California community college was found— in a site visit conducted by the lead author of this chapter—to be attracting students with master's degrees in biology.

Workforce Development for Low-Income Workers. The main alternative strategy for workforce development emerged from a consideration of the characteristics of the people who most need community college education. The low-income worker strategy views community colleges as institutions that can lift low-income workers out of poverty (Grubb, Badway, and Bell, 2003; Prince and Jenkins, 2005).

Some community colleges have established very successful programs using this approach. Northern Virginia Community College has collaborated with local medical providers to have adult basic education feed into allied health degree programs. Similarly, Tacoma Community College has integrated its English as a Second Language and early childhood programs to help students earn credits toward a degree in child care. All of these innovations benefit low-wage workers by helping them increase their wages and become upwardly mobile in the job market (National Council for Workforce Education and Jobs for the Future, 2004).

The design elements of this strategy are well-known. First, because many students cannot enter occupational classes until they improve their basic education skills, noncredit programs must be designed to allow adults to move easily into college credit programs. Second, the curriculum should be related to specific occupational fields, because low-income adults are primarily interested in college as a means to a better job. Third, support services must not stop at a specific literacy level, but should instead focus on helping students enter degree programs. Adult basic education thus becomes a feeder system for the community college's credit-based occupational programs.

A community college focus on low-skill, low-wage workers has been enthusiastically welcomed by educational foundations, yet this strategy has not received much response from community college leaders. One of the main concerns is that noncredit adult education programs require large amounts of resources, which is especially problematic when colleges are suffering significant cutbacks from state governments. Moreover, although many community colleges possess extensive basic education and English as a Second Language programs, these are often disconnected from the rest of the institution (Grubb, Badway, and Bell, 2003; Matus-Grossman and Gooden, 2002).

Conclusion

Many missions expected from the community college

Community colleges have historically played a great role in workforce preparation. However, workforce education has coexisted rather uneasily with other missions of the community college, such as transfer and general education, and faces several challenges. As we have seen, two somewhat contradictory strategies are being advocated to meet these challenges. Proponents of a new vocationalism argue that community colleges ought to prepare individuals for high-tech jobs in computer technologies, teaching, and health care, whereas others advocate for a renewed focus on meeting the needs of low-income workers.

Community college leaders are confused about which strategy to follow in good part because they are unclear about the future of the occupational labor market. According to labor economists, the *stair step* job growth of the past, which created more jobs at higher wages and fewer at lower wages, has been replaced with a *U-shaped* pattern of employment growth. Indeed, projections from the Bureau of Labor Statistics indicate that of the fifteen predicted fastest-growing occupations in the 2002–12 decade, six are in the lowest income quintile and only three are in the highest income quintile (Hecker, 2005).

For community colleges, whose occupational programs are frequently directed at training for jobs in the middle-income bracket, these developments pose great quandaries. Which occupational niches should colleges target, given that most of the high-income occupations require a baccalaureate or higher degree? If community colleges dismantle their current occupational programs and become primarily transfer institutions, will they lose their ability to reach out to the growing number of individuals in low-wage retail and commercial sectors? Yet, if community colleges promote education and training for lower-wage positions that may have higher rates of unemployment, will they actually reinforce social inequality?

The best way to avoid such dilemmas would be for colleges to create a vertically and horizontally integrated system of workforce training that stretches from noncredit adult education through the baccalaureate. Training programs should be connected vertically, so that students pursuing programs providing lesser skills or short-term training can later enter programs offering higher skills, longer training, and more valued certificates or degrees. Training programs should also be integrated horizontally, with trainees exposed—as needed—to various kinds of knowledge, including technical skills, academic skills, adult basic or remedial education, and job search and career guidance skills (Grubb, 1996).

References

American Association of Community Colleges. *The Knowledge Net.* Washington, D.C.: Community College Press, 2000.

Austin, J. "A Matter of Degrees." Paper presented at Community College Research Center Seminar, New York, Apr. 2005.

Bailey, T. R., Badway, N., and Gumport, P. *For-Profit Higher Education and Community Colleges.* Stanford, Calif.: Stanford University, National Center for Postsecondary Improvement, 2001.

Bartlett, K. *The Preconceived Influence of Industry-Sponsored Credentials in the Information Technology Industry.* Minneapolis: National Center for Career and Technical Education, 2002.

Bragg, D. D. (ed.). *The New Vocationalism in Community Colleges.* New Directions for Community Colleges, no. 115. San Francisco: Jossey-Bass, 2001.

Brint, S. G., and Karabel, J. B. *The Diverted Dream.* New York: Oxford University Press, 1989.

Carnevale, A., and Fry, R. *The Economic and Demographic Roots of Education and Training.* Washington, D.C.: National Association of Manufacturers, Center for Workforce Success, 2002.

Deil-Amen, R., and Rosenbaum, J. "The Social Prerequisites of Success: Can College Structure Reduce the Need for Social Know-How?" *Annals of the American Academy of Political and Social Science,* 2003, *586,* 120–143.

Dougherty, K. J. *The Contradictory College.* Albany: State University of New York Press, 1994.

Dougherty, K. J., and Bakia, M. F. "Community Colleges and Contract Training." *Teachers College Record,* 2000, *102*(1), 197–243.

Dougherty, K. J., and Kienzl, G. S. "It's Not Enough to Get Through the Open Door: Inequalities by Social Background in Transfer from Community Colleges to Four-Year Colleges." *Teachers College Record,* 2006, *108*(3), 452–487.

Dougherty, K. J., Reid, M., and Nienhusser, H. K. *State Policies to Achieve the Dream in Five States: An Audit of State Policies to Aid Student Access to and Success in Community Colleges in the First Five Achieving the Dream States.* New York: Columbia University, Teachers College, Community College Research Center, 2006. http://www.achievingthedream.org/_images/_index03/State_Pol_to_Achieve_Dream_5_States_2–27–06.pdf. Accessed Aug. 18, 2006.

Government Accounting Office. *Public Community Colleges and Technical Schools: Most Schools Use Both Credit and Non-Credit Programs for Workforce Development.* Washington, D.C.: Government Printing Office, 2005.

Grubb, W. N. *Working in the Middle.* San Francisco: Jossey-Bass, 1996.

Grubb, W. N., Badway, N., and Bell, D. "Community Colleges and the Equity Agenda: The Potential of Non-Credit Education." *Annals of the American Academy of Social and Political Science,* 2003, *586,* 218–240.

Grubb, W. N. Badway, N., Bell, D., Bragg, D. D., and Russman, M. *Workforce, Economic, and Community Development: The Changing Landscape of the Entrepreneurial Community College.* Phoenix: League for Innovation in the Community College, 1997.

Hecker, D. E. "Occupational Employment Projections to 2014." *Monthly Labor Review,* 2005, *128*(11), 70–101. http://www.bls.gov/opub/mlr/2005/11/art5full.pdf. Accessed Aug. 18, 2006.

Hughes, K. *Policy Implications of the Community College Transition Initiative.* New York: Columbia University, Teachers College, Community College Research Center, 2006.

Ignash, J. M., and Kotun, D. "Results of a National Study of Transfer in Occupational/ Technical Degrees: Policies and Practices." *Journal of Applied Research in the Community College,* 2005, *12*(2), 109–120.

Jacobs, J. "Community Colleges and the Workforce Investment Act: Promises and Problems of the New Vocationalism." In D. D. Bragg (ed.), *The New Vocationalism in Community Colleges.* New Directions for Community Colleges, no. 115. San Francisco: Jossey-Bass, 2001.

Jacobs, J., and Grubb, W. N. "Informational Technology and Skills Certification Programs in Community Colleges." In T. R. Bailey and V. S. Morest (eds.), *Defending the Community College Equity Agenda.* Baltimore: Johns Hopkins University Press, 2006.

Jacobs, J., and Teahen, R. *Shadow Colleges and NCA Accreditation: A Conceptual Framework.* Papers on Self-Study and Institutional Improvement. Chicago: North Central Association, 1996.

Karp, M. M., Jacobs, J., and Hughes, K. *Credentials, Curriculum, and Access: The Debate Over Nursing Preparation.* Washington, D.C.: Community College Press, 2002.

Matus-Grossman, L. M., and Gooden, S. *Opening Doors: Expanding Educational Opportunities for Low-Income Workers.* New York: Manpower Demonstration Research Corporation, 2002.

National Council for Workforce Education and Jobs for the Future. *Breaking Through: Helping Low-Skilled Adults Enter and Succeed in College and Careers.* Boston: Jobs for the Future, 2004.

National Governors Association. *Aligning State Workforce Development and Economic Development Initiatives.* Washington, D.C.: National Governors Association, NGA Center for Best Practices, 2005.

Prince, D., and Jenkins, D. *Building Pathways to Success for Low-Skill Adult Students* (CCRC Brief No. 25). New York: Columbia University, Teachers College, Community College Research Center, 2005.

Rosenfeld, S., Jacobs, J., and Liston, C. *"Clusters and Competencies": Workforce Development and South Carolina's Economy.* Carrboro, N.C.: Regional Technology Strategies, 2004. http://www.rtsinc.org/publications/SCReport.pdf. Accessed Aug. 18, 2006.

Shaw, K., and Goldrick-Rab, S. "Market Rhetoric Versus Reality in Policy and Practice: The Workforce Investment Act and Access to Community College Education and Training." *Annals of the American Academy of Political and Social Science,* 2003, *586,* 172–193.

Spence, R., and Kiel, B. *Skilling the American Workforce "on the Cheap."* Washington, D.C.: The Workforce Alliance, 2003.

Teles, E. "Advanced Technological Education." Paper presented at the Community College Research Center Seminar, New York, Nov. 2005.

JAMES JACOBS is director of the Center for Workforce Development and Policy at Macomb Community College and associate director for community college operations at the Community College Research Center at Teachers College, Columbia University.

KEVIN J. DOUGHERTY is associate professor of higher education and senior researcher at the Community College Research Center at Teachers College, Columbia University.

NEW DIRECTIONS FOR COMMUNITY COLLEGES • DOI: 10.1002/cc

7

With large numbers of underprepared students enrolling at community colleges, faculty are beginning to recognize that developmental education is a collegewide responsibility that needs to be fully integrated with the college's broader curriculum and varied missions.

Emerging Institutional Support for Developmental Education

Carol A. Kozeracki, J. Bryan Brooks

Developmental education, also known as remedial or preparatory education, holds a vital but often ill-defined place among community college curricular missions. Two national surveys conducted by the U.S. Department of Education (1996, 2003) indicate that between 98 and 100 percent of community colleges offer developmental courses in English, math, or reading and that more than 40 percent of entering freshmen at community colleges enroll in one or more of these courses. Cohen and Brawer (2003) confirm that developmental education is one of the central curricular functions of community colleges, along with academic transfer preparation, vocational-technical education, continuing education, and community service. However, developmental education differs fundamentally from these other curricular missions.

Unlike the other missions, which largely target specific student populations with shared long-term goals, developmental education is rarely an end in itself. Few students enroll in a community college with the stated goal of improving their basic academic skills. They take these courses as an initial step on a path elsewhere. Therefore, students' success should be measured by their ability to move from developmental courses to college-level courses and then to achieve success in transfer or vocational programs of study.

The open admissions policy of most community colleges means that few content courses outside of English and math have prerequisites. Thus, faculty in a wide range of disciplines and programs who have no background or training in working with underprepared students are often

NEW DIRECTIONS FOR COMMUNITY COLLEGES, no. 136, Winter 2006 © 2006 Wiley Periodicals, Inc.
Published online in Wiley InterScience (www.interscience.wiley.com) • DOI: 10.1002/cc.260

required to teach students who lack the necessary reading, writing, or mathematical skills to succeed. Ironically, the identification of developmental education as a separate mission of the college, and many institutions' choice to centralize their developmental programs, may contribute to the isolation of these programs, and, inadvertently intensify the chasm between college-level and developmental programs, both in terms of faculty ownership and student success.

Fortunately, there is increasing evidence that community colleges—often in response to recommendations or guidelines set out by accrediting commissions—are beginning to look at developmental education in a more inclusive way, recognizing that it takes place not only in precollege English and mathematics courses, but in many introductory (and even advanced) courses across the curriculum. In 1993, Roueche and Roueche warned, "Community colleges are so tightly enmeshed in developmental education that no one faculty member or department can afford to see himself or itself as outside of the problem" (p. 71). In the twenty-first century, colleges are now heeding that advice and beginning to creatively explore a range of collegewide organizational, programmatic, and professional development strategies to meet the needs of the many underprepared students.

For example, the faculty and staff of Davidson County Community College (DCCC) in North Carolina began an extensive self-analysis of how they were addressing the needs of their underprepared students in the late 1990s. During this process, they experienced an "aha!" moment in which they realized, "The underprepared students weren't problems that needed to be weeded out so we could get back to the business of teaching 'college' courses. They were our students, and their success became our mission" (*Strategic Study Report,* 2002, p. vi). DCCC's experience in redefining its approach to developmental education illustrates the holistic thinking and planning processes that lead to creative solutions for developmental students. This chapter examines the evolving role and organization of developmental education at community colleges, underscores the critical role that faculty from *all* disciplines must play if underprepared students are to succeed, and describes the journey undertaken by one college to change faculty and staff attitudes about developmental education policies and effectively integrate developmental education into the culture and mission of the institution.

Evolving Role and Structure of Developmental Education

Developmental education is defined in the context of the institution in which it is taught. The U.S. Department of Education (1996) uses the following definition: "Courses in reading, writing, or mathematics for college students lacking those skills necessary to perform college-level work at the level required by the institution" (p. 2). According to this definition, what constitutes developmental education varies from institution to institution.

NEW DIRECTIONS FOR COMMUNITY COLLEGES • DOI: 10.1002/cc

Developmental education program requirements and content are influenced by institutional mission regarding transfer and workforce preparation, quality of service-area high schools, demographics of the student population, articulation agreements with universities, employer expectations as voiced through advisory committees and employer surveys, regional and program-specific accreditation requirements, and accountability standards such as licensure pass rates, placement rates, and graduation rates.

In defining developmental education, it is entirely appropriate to consider the long-term intended outcomes of a community college education, given how few students identify attaining a level of competence in basic skills as their goal for attending a community college. For example, of the more than 113,000 students who enrolled in the Los Angeles Community College District in fall 2005, less than 3 percent listed "improving basic skills in English/reading/math" as their main educational goal, compared to 31 percent who identified transfer and 35 percent who specified career-related preparation (Los Angeles Community College District, 2005). Although many of these students will require developmental courses in English and math as part of their course work, they are likely to view these classes as a means to an end—necessary, but often undesired, prerequisites for a vocational or transfer program. Under this scenario, the *primary* purpose of developmental programs is to facilitate students' transition from remedial to college-level courses, and to improve students' chances of success in transfer and vocational programs. This purpose requires that developmental courses be fully integrated into the broader community college curriculum.

Unfortunately, the structure of developmental programs at many community colleges, and the failure of these programs to help students progress through college-level courses, may isolate developmental instruction from the broader college curriculum. Indeed, there are long-standing debates about whether to centralize developmental education into a distinct department or integrate it into existing academic divisions. Creating a separate department tends to increase the likelihood that the college will hire faculty who are primarily interested in and trained to work with underprepared students, and it makes it easier to coordinate the range of important support services these students require (Boylan, 2002; Perin, 2005). The disadvantage of centralization is that interaction between developmental faculty and college-level instructors in math and English may be limited. As a result, exit standards for the developmental courses may not be properly aligned with the skills required to succeed in college-level classes. Furthermore, some researchers warn that separation creates a secondary instructional program. Grubb (1999) states: "Remediation is a low-status activity, the custodial or housekeeping department of college-level instruction. . . . Within community colleges, remediation is usually organized as an activity separate from the core purposes, isolated in a jigsaw puzzle of developmental reading and writing departments and tutorial programs" (pp. 171–172).

This organizational divide between developmental and college-level courses is reflected in the large number of students who are placed into developmental classes but never move on to complete more advanced college courses. The National Study of Community College Remedial Education (McCabe, 2000) discovered that nearly half of community college remedial students successfully complete their program, but found much worse results for "seriously deficient students" (p. 36), who required remediation in reading, writing, and mathematics. A statewide study conducted by the California Community College Chancellor's Office (2005) found that only 27 percent of more than 650,000 students who enrolled in basic skills courses in 2001–02 had enrolled in and successfully completed a higher-level course in the same subject by 2004. A similar study in North Carolina revealed that 22 percent of basic skills students advanced to a higher level in 2003–04 (North Carolina Community College System, 2005).

Even if many of the students placed into developmental courses do not successfully move on to college-level courses in English and math, they often are able to enroll in other subject areas without a prerequisite. As a result, community college faculty who do not officially teach developmental classes often face underprepared students in their classes. Grubb (1999) categorizes this as remediation in disguise: "Remediation takes place in many other guises, in classes not listed in course catalogues as remedial. These are often classes with ad hoc remediation, as instructors discover the need to detour into subjects that they might ordinarily expect college-level students to know" (p. 194). According to the most recent faculty survey by the Higher Education Research Institute (Lindholm, Szelenyi, Hurtado, and Korn, 2005), 65 percent of community college faculty agree somewhat or strongly that "most of the students I teach lack the basic skills for college-level work" (p. 41). At these same institutions, 68 percent of the faculty report at least some level of stress associated with working with underprepared students. This statistic is all the more striking, given that three-quarters of the respondents to this survey were not teaching a developmental class during the semester the survey was administered.

Clearly, developmental education is not confined to a limited number of precollege reading, English, and math courses. Both trained developmental instructors and content instructors with no formal background in working with underprepared students teach students with limited academic preparation and skills. Therefore, colleges need to develop organizational and instructional models that bring together the benefits of department-based and centralized developmental education. Cohen and Brawer (2003) assert that community colleges "that have erected separate programs that concentrate exclusively on remedial studies . . . are effective only when they are comprehensive efforts complete with support services and connections with the colleges' other programs" (p. 279). Central Florida Community College, for example, recently created a position for an associate dean with the primary responsibility of coordinating the various services being provided for underprepared students. This individual works with faculty leaders from four key departments—English, reading, math, and college success (also known as freshman study skills)—who have been given release time for curriculum development and evaluation. This organizational approach, which brings together the experience and focus of a central developmental education expert and faculty leaders' department-based knowledge and connections, has tremendous promise for assisting the college's developmental students (*College Success Initiative*, 2005). *Good pt! Resources are needed*

A number of researchers assert the need for an institutional commitment to developmental education if it is to succeed (Boylan, 2002; Roueche and Roueche, 1993). Although institutional commitment is generally perceived as high-level administrative support and the availability of financial resources, these are insufficient if there is not extensive faculty involvement and commitment throughout the campus. If many instructors long for the good old days when students took their studies seriously, or if they feel that teaching students to write well is the exclusive domain of the English department, then developmental programs are not likely to succeed. Depending on the history of a campus, the longevity of the faculty, and the evolving demographics of the students, the acceptance and embrace of an often underprepared student population may be a slow and painful process.

A number of campuses have delved into the needs of their students, garnered the strong support and ongoing involvement of staff and faculty, and created comprehensive developmental programs. In 2004, twenty-seven community colleges were funded by the Lumina Foundation for Education as part of their Achieving the Dream: Community Colleges Count project that supports community colleges in their efforts to foster student success, particularly among low-income students and students of color. Of these twenty-seven institutions, twenty-one specifically identified developmental courses as a collegewide focus for their project (www.achievingthedream. org). Developmental programs at these colleges are being integrated into the academic and social mainstream, thus avoiding the punitive, low-status overtones and the "you cure them" mentality connoted by isolation in a separate remedial department (Keimig, 1983, p. 15).

In addition to the influence of external funding, regional accreditation and accountability efforts have also contributed to the evolution of developmental education as a college focus. Davidson County Community College (DCCC) in North Carolina, for example, has engaged in a multiple-year process that involved dozens of faculty and staff members serving on task forces to explore the background and progress of their students. They investigated best practices in developmental education and designed strategies and programs to address the needs of their underprepared students. DCCC's engaging and highly participatory process helped foster an institutionalized commitment to the success of underprepared students.

Reenvisioning Developmental Education at Davidson County Community College

As in many other states, a significant number of North Carolina's graduating high school seniors must enroll in developmental classes once they enter a community college. Between 1996–97 and 2003–04, the percent of the state's high school graduates who took one or more developmental courses at a community college within one year of graduating rose from 40.2 to 49.2 percent, reaching a high of 54.3 percent in 2001–02. At Davidson County Community College, a comprehensive institution that enrolled 4,268 students in 2003–04, the number of students enrolled in developmental courses increased by 50 percent between 1997 and 2003 (see Table 7.1).

At the time DCCC began preparing for its 2002 accreditation visit, there were conflicting views about the role of and approach to developmental education on the campus. Many faculty felt that current students were less qualified than in past years and argued that standards should not be lowered in order to accommodate underprepared students. Others were committed to meeting the needs of all students who enrolled.

During early discussions about how to shape the college's accreditation self-study, a group of faculty and staff responsible for selecting the focus of the alternate model self-study agreed on several criteria. First, the topic must be of great importance to the learning process. Second, it should involve a significant cross section of the institution, and there should be collegewide involvement in creating the strategic plan to address the issue. Third, there must be a clear vision of how the college would change as a result of the study. Finally, the process must be manageable and affordable, and the results measurable.

Developmental education was selected not only because it cut across most programs and services at the college, but also because a number of concerns related to the topic had already been identified. First, there had been a dramatic increase in the number of underprepared students enrolling at the college in recent years. There was also a concern that the develop-

Table 7.1. Developmental Course Offerings and Enrollment at Davidson County Community College

Academic Year	Number of Developmental Course Sections	Number of Students Enrolled
1997–98	62	1,044
1998–99	71	1,202
1999–2000	67	1,223
2000–01	71	1,198
2001–02	76	1,512
2002–03	79	1,598

Source: Davidson County Community College.

NEW DIRECTIONS FOR COMMUNITY COLLEGES • DOI: 10.1002/cc

mental courses did not create a sound foundation for success in college-level courses and programs. As well, faculty and staff were aware that a disproportionate amount of time and resources were being dedicated to the placement and advising of underprepared students. In addition, a number of projects conducted by the college in the mid-1990s had helped familiarize faculty with how to teach to students'—especially developmental students'—learning styles.

After several months of committee work on the project, DCCC hired an external consultant, an expert in developmental education from Appalachian State University, to visit the campus and evaluate its existing program and enhancement plans. Based on this individual's recommendations, the college developed subcommittees to explore the following areas: advisement, assessment, coordination and learning support, communication, evaluation, and curriculum and development. Almost thirty faculty members, chairs, deans, and administrators served on these subcommittees. Each group was given a charge and a series of related issues to address. In response, they provided their findings and a set of conclusions on the topic, which laid the groundwork for new programs and services. The institutional use of effective group processes, data gathering, collaboration, informed decision making, and a genuine commitment to search for and employ state-of-the-art practices, contributed to the transformation of this institution.

The advisement committee highlighted the need for advising to take place as soon as possible after each student's first assessment, and for advisors to be able to "articulate tactfully and accurately" the requirements of a developmental program (*Strategic Study Report,* 2002, p. 56). It also recommended that advising be part of the Learning Assistance Center, which the college was considering establishing, and that advisors continually update their knowledge about changes in the advisement process. Finally, this subcommittee stressed the importance of faculty providing feedback to students early in the semester in order to maximize student success in developmental and other classes.

The assessment subcommittee, which was charged with evaluating assessment policies and practices related to preparatory studies, confirmed that students who score below the lowest placement benchmark for entry into preparatory courses undergo some type of basic skills intervention. The committee also recommended that the benchmarks for a variety of assessment instruments be examined for consistency and compatibility.

The coordination and learning support subcommittee examined the purpose of developmental studies at the college, their compatibility with the college's broad mission, and the appropriate organizational structure of the program. The preparatory education mission statement—"College preparatory education includes comprehensive services and programs which promote the success of all students in moving from an entry level of achievement toward successful completion of the chosen program of study" (*Strategic Study Report,* 2002, p. 60)—was deemed to be a good match with the college's mission statement because it described taking students from where they were at entry and helping them realize their goals for enhanced employment or further education. Faculty and staff fully recognized that preparatory education was not merely an isolated service provided to a few underprepared students but rather an integral part of the college's mission. They also decided that a hybrid organizational model, in which developmental courses are housed in their own disciplines but support services and other activities are centrally coordinated, would be most appropriate for DCCC.

Charged with reviewing developmental courses to determine the consistency of course expectations and exit criteria, the preparatory studies curriculum and development subcommittee found that there was no general list of expectations for students in all preparatory classes. It also found that although all courses met specified exit criteria, some faculty added requirements, which resulted in inconsistent standards. The subcommittee recommended that all these courses adhere to a general list of expectations including such items as classroom behavior, homework and grading policies, and academic integrity.

The evaluation subcommittee conducted a substantial amount of internal research: comparing students not needing preparatory work with students who placed into developmental classes, exploring student retention rates in a number of preparatory classes, examining student success in subsequent courses, and analyzing student grades and outcomes. Committee members were pleased to find that close to one-third of the 389 students earning a degree, diploma, or certificate from DCCC in the 1999–2000 academic year had taken at least one preparatory class. However, they also discovered that a number of students who tested into developmental courses had graduated without meeting these requirements. Consequently, the committee recommended that the college investigate these loopholes.

After evaluating the effectiveness of the campus in sharing information about developmental education with faculty, staff, and students, the communications subcommittee realized that faculty were not using similar formats to create syllabi for developmental classes, making it more difficult for students to understand course expectations and outcomes. The committee also realized that some of the language the college was using to discuss developmental education carried negative connotations. They concluded that "assessment," "benchmarks," and "preparatory studies" were more positively perceived by students than "testing," "cut scores," and "developmental education."

Following several more months of work by the groups, another external consultant—an expert in the first-year college experience—was invited to DCCC to conduct an assessment and offer additional recommendations for enhancing the college's programs and services. With these substantial findings and recommendations across a range of areas, the college was awarded a TRIO grant to help institute many of the recommended changes. Among the most important was the creation of four new positions to help foster success among preparatory students: a counselor to work directly with preparatory students; a director of admissions and records, who would focus on reframing the assessment process to make it smoother for students; a coordinator for the TRIO program to oversee the provision of advising, tutoring, transfer information, workshops, and cultural events; and a learning support coordinator to manage services for preparatory students. Among the learning support coordinator's responsibilities was the newly established Learning Assistance Center, which began offering supplemental instruction, a writing center, free tutoring, study skills workshops, and computer access for students. Ongoing faculty development workshops have touched on areas such as working with students with disabilities, advising, and syllabus creation.

Perhaps the most dramatic outcome of DCCC's collaborative process was the change in faculty attitudes. Between July 1999, when a cross-functional group decided to focus the college's accreditation self-study on preparing students for college-level work, and fall 2001, when the strategic plan was completed, a transformation occurred. Although many faculty were previously nostalgic for earlier generations of better-prepared students, they evolved into a group that was fully committed to working with all students who enrolled at DCCC. "As long as there are students who need our assistance to be successful, we will continue to learn, to try, and to evaluate new methods of enhancing their learning. After all, these *are* our students" (*Strategic Study Report,* 2002, p. v). Faculty and staff realized that serving underprepared students was essential to the core purpose of their college and that these services involved most departments and programs. When faculty and staff stopped arguing about the quality of past students and decided to collaborate and create a developmental education program that would effectively serve the needs of current and future students, everyone benefited. A new commitment to helping every student succeed became part of the shared vision of the college.

Conclusion

National studies (Grubb, 1999; U.S. Department of Education, 1996, 2003) demonstrate that developmental education—both official and "in disguise"—constitutes a substantial portion of the community college curriculum, and that many community college students would be unable to meet their goals without this important intervention. Across the country, state legislatures are enacting laws requiring community colleges to take on an increased share of remedial instruction (Jenkins and Boswell, 2002), ensuring that this role will not decrease or vanish in the foreseeable future. In response, community colleges can choose different approaches to address underprepared students' needs and facilitate their growth and progress. One approach is to rely on the faculty who teach developmental courses to bring these students up to speed. An alternative approach is to recognize that faculty at all levels and in all disciplines have underprepared students in their classes, and ask them to play a role in ensuring the success of these students.

A broad-based commitment to developmental education is being made at individual community colleges across the country (*College Success Initiative,* 2005; Lake, 2002). Recently, the Academic Senate for California Community Colleges (2003) came to the conclusion that "local senates should lead their faculty and administration to view basic skills instruction as central to the community college mission . . . [and] should lead the college to take a more global approach to the instruction of basic skills students so that faculty from all areas participate in an 'across-the-curriculum' approach to basic skills learners" (p. 22). Widespread institutional support for developmental education programs—as manifested in consistent administrative support, sufficient financial resources, and pervasive faculty involvement—can help improve the outcomes of students who are most in need of the assistance and support that community colleges are willing and able to provide.

References

Academic Senate for California Community Colleges. *A Survey of Best Practices in Basic Skills.* Sacramento: Academic Senate for California Community Colleges, 2003.

Boylan, H. R. *What Works: Research-Based Best Practices in Developmental Education.* Boone, N.C.: Continuous Quality Improvement Network with the National Center for Developmental Education, 2002.

California Community College Chancellor's Office. *System Performance on Partnership for Excellence Indicators.* Sacramento: California Community College Chancellor's Office, 2005.

Cohen, A. M., and Brawer, F. B. *The American Community College.* (4th ed.) San Francisco: Jossey-Bass, 2003.

College Success Initiative: Preparing Students for College Level Learning. Ocala: Central Florida Community College, 2005.

Grubb, W. N. *Honored But Invisible: An Inside Look at Teaching in Community Colleges.* New York: Routledge, 1999.

Jenkins, D., and Boswell, K. *State Policies on Community College Remedial Education: Findings from a National Survey.* Denver: Education Commission of the States, 2002.

Keimig, R. *Raising Academic Standards: A Guide to Learning Improvement* (ASHE/ERIC Higher Education Research Report No. 4). Washington, D.C.: Association for the Study of Higher Education, 1983.

Lake, P. R. (ed.). "A Centralized Approach to Developmental Education: A Collegewide Strategy for Student Success." *Southern Association of Community, Junior, and Technical Colleges Newsletter,* 2002, 37(1), 4–16.

Lindholm, J. A., Szelenyi, K., Hurtado, S., and Korn, W. S. *The American College Teacher: National Norms for the 2004–2005 HERI Faculty Survey.* Los Angeles: University of California, Los Angeles Higher Education Research Institute, 2005.

Los Angeles Community College District. *Enrollment by Educational Goal, Fall 1983–Fall 2005.* Los Angeles: Los Angeles Community College District, 2005. http://research.laccd.edu/enrollment-trends/index.htm. Accessed Nov. 18, 2005.

McCabe, R. H. *No One to Waste: A Report to Public Decision Makers and Community College Leaders.* Washington, D.C.: Community College Press, 2000.

North Carolina Community College System. *2005 Critical Success Factors (16th Annual Report).* Raleigh: North Carolina Community College System, Office of Planning, Accountability, Research, and Evaluation, 2005.

Perin, D. "Institutional Decision Making for Increasing Academic Preparedness in Community Colleges." In C. A. Kozeracki (ed.), *Responding to the Challenges of Developmental Education*. New Directions for Community Colleges, no. 129. San Francisco: Jossey-Bass, 2005.

Roueche, J. E., and Roueche, S. D. *Between a Rock and a Hard Place: The At-Risk Student in the Open-Door Classroom*. Washington, D.C.: Community College Press, 1993.

Strategic Study Report: Essential Skills for Lifelong Learning. Lexington, N.C.: Davidson County Community College, 2002.

U.S. Department of Education, National Center for Education Statistics. *Remedial Education at Higher Education Institutions in Fall 1995* (NCES 97–584). Washington, D.C.: U.S. Department of Education, 1996.

U.S. Department of Education, National Center for Education Statistics. *Remedial Education at Degree-Granting Postsecondary Institutions in Fall 2000* (Statistical Analysis Report No. 2004–010). Washington, D.C.: U.S. Department of Education, 2003.

CAROL A. KOZERACKI is associate dean of research, planning, and assessment at Los Angeles Pierce College.

J. BRYAN BROOKS is chair of the Department of Leadership and Educational Studies at Appalachian State University in North Carolina.

8

Continuing education divisions in community colleges tend to be among the most entrepreneurial and innovative programs in higher education. This chapter presents data from a national survey of continuing education programs and suggests that shifting economic and institutional factors influence the manner in which community colleges offer those programs.

Competing Missions: Balancing Entrepreneurialism with Community Responsiveness in Community College Continuing Education Divisions

John A. Downey, Brian Pusser, J. Kirsten Turner

Continuing education programs offering credit and noncredit courses, certificates, and degrees now constitute an integral aspect of the mission of many community colleges in the United States. One of the least understood community college functions, continuing education can be defined broadly as the range of programs and services that provide workforce training, adult basic education, academic transfer curricula, personal enrichment, and community outreach courses.

Long considered an auxiliary aspect of postsecondary organizations, continuing education divisions at community colleges serve an increasingly diverse group of learners in their local communities, as well as through state and national partnerships. These entities often generate surplus revenues in the process. As a result, community college continuing education divisions have been described as some of the more entrepreneurial postsecondary education programs (Pusser, Gansneder, Gallaway, and Pope, 2005).

Despite their prominence in the community colleges, little empirical research has been conducted on continuing education programs and the students who enroll in them. This chapter draws on data collected by the Emerging Pathways project, a national study of adult and nontraditional learners in postsecondary education that is supported by the Lumina Foundation for Education. Here, we present a range of activities that fall under

NEW DIRECTIONS FOR COMMUNITY COLLEGES, no. 136, Winter 2006 © 2006 Wiley Periodicals, Inc.
Published online in Wiley InterScience (www.interscience.wiley.com) • DOI: 10.1002/cc.261

the category of continuing education and explore them in light of their contributions to the traditional community college missions of open access and community responsiveness.

Data Source

The data reported in this chapter are drawn from the Emerging Pathways project, a longitudinal research initiative based in the Center for the Study of Higher Education at the University of Virginia. The Emerging Pathways project focuses on the study of adult learners and nontraditional students in innovative pathways to degrees, credentials, and training (Pusser, Gansneder, Gallaway, and Pope, 2005). As part of this research, a survey was provided to a random sample of 524 community colleges, stratified by state. Of the 524 institutions sampled, 226 (43.1 percent) returned the surveys. Comparisons with available Integrated Postsecondary Education Data System (IPEDS) characteristics revealed no significant differences between the initial sample and the returned sample in terms of the percentage of tribal colleges, degree of urbanization, percent of American Indian or Alaskan students, and percent of Hispanic or black students. However, four significant differences were found. Compared to the initial sample, the returned sample included more public institutions (91.9 versus 85.5 percent), fewer schools with total enrollment under 1,499 students (21.1 versus 33.8 percent), and more Asian/Pacific Islander students (27.4 versus 21.8 percent). The returned sample also included a greater number of schools in which more than 60 percent of the student body was nonwhite (Center for the Study of Higher Education, 2005).

Course Offerings

Data from the Emerging Pathways project indicate that there are four primary types of course offerings in community college continuing education divisions: workforce development courses that are designed to develop workplace readiness skills but generally do not lead to a certificate or credential; credit-bearing general education and transfer preparation courses that lead to an associate degree or transfer to a four-year institution; noncredit professional education courses that lead to a certificate, professional license, or industry-recognized credential; and noncredit community service, general interest, and leisure courses. We discuss each of these types of continuing education course offerings in the following sections.

Skill and Workforce Development Courses. The close proximity of community colleges to local business and industry has allowed continuing education divisions to emerge as a significant provider of workforce development training services (Drury, 2001). Community colleges also play a significant role in providing adult basic education, now estimated to constitute approximately 15 percent of community college noncredit enrollments (Morest, 2004). Continuing education divisions often offer both credit and noncredit workforce training courses, and usually tailor such courses to meet the needs of local businesses. In the survey, 78.7 percent of continuing education divisions reported developing courses and certificate programs in partnership with local governments over the past four years, and 58.1 percent have entered into such agreements with state governments. Nonetheless, the majority of financial support for workforce training courses continues to come from businesses that sponsor training for their employees.

The most common type of skill and workforce courses continuing education divisions offer for credit include those in health services (47.1 percent of the colleges in our survey offered courses in this area), computer and information technologies (47.1 percent), and business management (44.3 percent). Computer and information technology is the most common noncredit offering (82.9 of surveyed colleges offered noncredit courses in this area). As well, 38.6 percent of surveyed colleges reported offering noncredit adult basic education courses (Center for the Study of Higher Education, 2005).

Transfer Credit Courses and Programs. Our survey also demonstrates that a significant number of community college continuing education divisions offer credit courses in areas traditionally associated with the academic transfer curriculum; 11.6 percent of surveyed colleges indicated that their continuing education program includes a transferable associate degree. Given the importance of providing more students with the knowledge and skills necessary to transfer and earn a bachelor's degree, a growing number of community college continuing education programs are developing courses that can transfer to a four-year institution.

Professional Education. Community colleges' continuing education divisions also offer opportunities for professional education, including training that leads directly to professional certificates, licenses, or other industry-recognized credentials. For example, many Virginia community college continuing education divisions are addressing the shortage of secondary math and science teachers by offering an innovative career preparation program that allows individuals with significant workforce experience and a bachelor's degree to become licensed teachers. Similarly, one community college in Washington State has launched a viticulture certification program that helps rural farmers in wine country soften the economic impact of declining profits from traditional crops (VanAusdle, 2005). Across the country, professional training programs, particularly in the information technology field, reflect growing demand from business and industry for industry-recognized certifications (Flynn, 2005).

General Interest Courses. Data from the Emerging Pathways survey also show that 29.5 percent of courses in community college continuing education divisions are general interest, lifelong learning courses such as amateur photography, ballroom dancing, or home gardening. Despite the perception that general interest courses may lack academic rigor, such courses can also play an important economic role in a local community by providing access to new technologies or by increasing awareness about local commerce. In addition, the diverse range of courses helps community colleges remain responsive to the needs of their local constituents and reflects the traditions, values, and attributes of those communities. Responsiveness to a local community is a key community college mission that also leads to additional budget allocations, philanthropic contributions, and political support (Bailey and Morest, 2004).

Common Characteristics of Continuing Education Offerings

Despite pressures to generate surplus revenue, the majority (77.5 percent) of continuing education courses have fewer than twenty students per course, which allows instruction to be tailored to students' needs. Continuing education courses are typically scheduled outside the confines of a traditional academic calendar. Most noncredit courses are offered in the evenings and on the weekends, although many credit courses are offered within the traditional academic schedule. As well, many noncredit continuing education courses do not require prerequisites, a minimum grade point average, or score on a competency exam. Continuing education divisions also tend to offer fewer academic support services to noncredit students than to those in credit classes. Approximately two-thirds of surveyed colleges offer remedial services to credit students; only 35.7 percent offer such services to noncredit students.

Institutional Goals for Continuing Education

Much has been written that suggests community colleges view responsiveness to workforce, community, and individual educational needs as an integral part of their mission (Levin, 2005). Survey respondents were asked to express the most important goals they hope to achieve through their continuing education program offerings. Over 62 percent of community college respondents ranked skill acquisition as either the most important or second most important goal when planning credit courses and programs in their continuing education divisions. For noncredit offerings, 39.2 percent of respondents ranked engaging with the community, 41.8 percent ranked providing skill acquisition, and 44.9 percent ranked promoting economic development as their most important or second most important goal. These findings suggest that helping students acquire specific skills is the primary motivation for continuing education credit instruction, and that community engagement is the primary goal for noncredit courses. These results indicate that strategic decisions made by continuing education practitioners about the types of courses offered are not based solely on whether such courses will generate income, but rather on the basis of multiple competing factors, as other research has suggested (Dougherty, 2003; Grubb, Badway, and Bell, 2003; Grubb, Badway, Bell, Bragg, and Russman, 1997; Johnstone, 1998).

Indeed, of surveyed institutions, 63.4 percent reported that institutional mission was the most important or the second most important factor when planning continuing education course offerings, and 32.5 percent ranked student demand as the third most important factor. Despite the perception that state and local governments are becoming more involved in continuing education and workforce development, 70.8 percent of continuing education divisions surveyed responded that government demands were the least important factor in their strategic planning. Taken collectively, these data suggest that—although there are competing pressures at play in strategic planning for continuing education divisions—responsiveness to the local community and ensuring open access for students remain priorities.

Challenges to the Continuing Education Function

Flexibility, innovation, and responsiveness have long been considered the hallmarks of continuing education in community colleges. However, myriad new internal and external factors pose significant obstacles for continuing education divisions. Two challenges are highlighted here: increased competition for dwindling revenue sources coupled with revenue constraints, and increased competition from for-profit educational institutions.

Competition for Dwindling Revenue Sources. Since the late 1970s, state funding for higher education has increased only modestly, even though operating costs have grown dramatically (Newman, Couturier, and Scurry, 2004). As a result, community colleges face increasing demands to become more efficient and to do more with less. As enrollments increase and demand grows for programs that provide labor market skills for a globalized economy (Levin, 2001), colleges must build and maintain larger, more complex, and expensive programs. Revenue constraints have resulted in institutional commitments to entrepreneurial approaches to resource generation, particularly in continuing education divisions (Pusser, Gansneder, Gallaway, and Pope, 2005). This focus on efficiency and entrepreneurialism may challenge efforts to preserve the community college's historical missions of open access and create conflict between continuing education programs that generate profits and those that provide courses for individual and community enrichment (Pusser and Doane, 2001).

Competition From the For-Profit Sector. Degree-granting for-profit postsecondary institutions have existed for many years, but have risen to greater prominence over the past two decades. Although they account for less than 5 percent of all postsecondary enrollments (Breneman, 2005; Breneman, Pusser, and Turner, forthcoming), their rapid growth has caused many nonprofit institutions to take notice. In 1966, 15 percent of postsecondary students were over the age of twenty-five. Three decades later, 43 percent were twenty-five or older (Collis, 1999). Degree-granting proprietary institutions such as the University of Phoenix capitalize on these shifting demographics by narrowly tailoring their courses and programs to older, working students and limiting expenses, particularly faculty compensation (Berg, 2005; Kirp, 2003). Outcalt and Schirmer (2003) argue that the narrow focus of proprietary institutions could pose a threat to community colleges that offer more comprehensive programs and services. Indeed, two-year proprietary schools are particularly assertive in enrolling adult students and providing them with assistance in seeking financial aid (Deil-Amen and Rosenbaum, 2003). However, community colleges have greater legitimacy and public support than for-profit institutions, and as long as community colleges continue to be responsive to demographic shifts, political and economic demands, and labor market opportunities, they will prosper in spite of competition from for-profit institutions. Indeed, given their history of success and current positioning, community college continuing education divisions appear to be well-poised to gain further comparative advantage over for-profit providers.

Conclusion

Continuing education programs can be seen as both supporting and challenging the primary missions of community colleges. Because they are entrepreneurial in nature, continuing education divisions are able to respond quickly to community needs. Given their supportive admission requirements, low fees, and commitment to convenient delivery of courses, these programs make a significant contribution to community colleges' access mission (Dougherty and Bakia, 2000). However, if entrepreneurial revenue generation becomes more important to institutional leaders than access, affordability, or programmatic diversity, the expansion of continuing education has the potential to infringe on the community college's core commitments.

Findings from the National Study of Continuing Education (Center for the Study of Higher Education, 2005) suggest that continuing education divisions are adapting to meet the challenges of increased competition, decreased funding, and widespread changes in educational delivery methods by fostering increased entrepreneurial activities and innovation. As well, most continuing education programs are endeavoring to balance revenue generation with allegiance to institutional mission. It appears that continuing education will play an increasingly important role in ensuring student access and success as community colleges adapt to a rapidly changing political economy for postsecondary education.

References

Bailey, T. R., and Morest, V. S. *The Organizational Efficiency of Multiple Missions for Community Colleges.* New York: Columbia University, Teachers College, Community College Research Center, 2004. http://ccrc.tc.columbia.edu/ContentByType.asp?t=1. Accessed Oct. 29, 2005.

Berg, G. A. *Lessons From the Edge: For-Profit and Non-Traditional Higher Education in America.* New York: Praeger, 2005.

Breneman, D. W. "All Sectors of Higher Education Have Become More Entrepreneurial in the Face of Political and Economic Pressures." In B. Pusser (ed.), *Arenas of Entrepreneurship: Where Non-Profit and For-Profit Institutions Compete.* New Directions for Higher Education, no. 129. San Francisco: Jossey-Bass, 2005.

Breneman, D. W., Pusser, B., and Turner, S. E. (eds.). *Earnings From Learning: The Rise of For-Profit Universities.* Albany: State University of New York Press, forthcoming.

Center for the Study of Higher Education. "Institutions: 2004 National Study on Continuing Education." Unpublished manuscript, University of Virginia, Charlottesville, 2005.

Collis, D. "When Industries Change Revisited: New Scenarios for Higher Education." Paper presented at the Forum for the Future of Higher Education, Aspen, Colo., Sept. 1999.

Deil-Amen, R., and Rosenbaum, J. "The Social Prerequisites of Success: Can College Structure Reduce the Need for Social Know-How?" *Annals of the American Academy of Political and Social Science,* 2003, *586,* 120–143.

Dougherty, K. J. "The Uneven Distribution of Employee Training by Community Colleges: Description and Explanation." *Annals of the American Academy of Political and Social Science,* 2003, *586,* 62–91.

Dougherty, K. J., and Bakia, M. F. "Community Colleges and Contract Training: Content, Origins, and Impact." *Teachers College Record,* 2000, *102*(1), 197–243.

Drury, R. L. "The Entrepreneurial Community College: Bringing Workforce, Economic and Community Development to Virginia Communities." *Inquiry: The Journal of the Virginia Community Colleges,* 2001, *6*(1), 26–33.

Flynn, W. *Eight Strategic Questions for Community Colleges.* Carlsbad, Calif.: National Consortium for Continuing Education and Training, 2005. http://www.nccet.org/associations/2158/SCTmonograph.pdf. Accessed Dec. 31, 2005.

Grubb, W. N., Badway, N., and Bell, D. "Community College and the Equity Agenda: The Potential of Noncredit Education." *Annals of the American Academy of Political and Social Science,* 2003, *586*(1), 218–240.

Grubb, W. N., Badway, N., Bell, D., Bragg, D. D., and Russman, M. *Workforce, Economic, and Community Development: The Changing Landscape of the "Entrepreneurial" Community College.* Phoenix: League for Innovation in the Community College, 1997.

Johnstone, D. B. "The Financing and Management of Higher Education: A Status Report on Worldwide Reforms." Paper presented at the UNESCO World Conference on Higher Education, Paris, France, Oct. 1998.

Kirp, D. L. *Shakespeare, Einstein and the Bottom Line.* Cambridge: Harvard University Press, 2003.

Levin, J. S. *Globalizing the Community College: Strategies for Change in the Twenty-First Century.* New York: Palgrave Macmillan, 2001.

Levin, J. S. "The Business Culture of the Community College: Students as Consumers; Students as Commodities." In B. Pusser (ed.), *Arenas of Entrepreneurship: Where Non-Profit and For-Profit Institutions Compete.* New Directions for Higher Education, no. 129. San Francisco: Jossey-Bass, 2005.

Morest, V. S. *The Role of Community Colleges in State Adult Education Systems: A National Analysis.* New York: Council for Advancement of Adult Literacy, 2004.

Newman, F., Couturier, L. K., and Scurry, J. *The Future of Higher Education: Rhetoric, Reality, and the Risks of the Market.* San Francisco: Jossey-Bass, 2004.

Outcalt, C. L., and Schirmer, J. E. "ERIC Review: Understanding the Relationships Between Proprietary Schools and Community Colleges: Findings from Recent Literature." *Community College Review,* 2003, *31*(1), 56–73.

Pusser, B., and Doane, D. "Public Purpose and Private Enterprise: The Contemporary Organization of Postsecondary Education." *Change,* 2001, *33*(5), 18–22.

Pusser, B., Gansneder, B. M., Gallaway, N., and Pope, N. S. "Entrepreneurial Activity in Nonprofit Institutions: A Portrait of Continuing Education." In B. Pusser (ed.), *Arenas of Entrepreneurship: Where Non-Profit and For-Profit Institutions Compete.* New Directions for Higher Education, no. 129. San Francisco: Jossey-Bass, 2005.

VanAusdle, S. L. "Changing Times for Rural Prosperity Through Wine, Food and Art." *Community College Journal,* 2005, 75(6), 10–14.

JOHN A. DOWNEY *is vice president for instruction and student services at Blue Ridge Community College in Weyers Cave, Virginia.*

BRIAN PUSSER *is assistant professor in the Center for the Study of Higher Education at the University of Virginia.*

J. KIRSTEN TURNER *is assistant dean for academic planning and analysis at the University of Kentucky.*

NEW DIRECTIONS FOR COMMUNITY COLLEGES • DOI: 10.1002/cc

9

Faced with growing pressure to demonstrate student success and achieve financial stability, community colleges have increasingly turned to enrollment management. Using Bronx Community College as an example, this chapter examines the role institutional research can play in the enrollment management process.

Enrollment Management in the Comprehensive Community College: A Case Study of Bronx Community College

Nancy Ritze

Recent national trends—such as loss of status as the most highly educated nation, increasing diversity of the U.S. population, gaps in educational attainment and economic prosperity between whites and minorities, and the underrepresentation of minorities at each level of education—point to the continued importance of addressing inequality in American postsecondary education. Comprehensive community colleges can function as vehicles to help redress some of these disturbing trends. The comprehensive community college plays multiple roles—providing transfer and vocational education, community outreach, and workforce development—while promoting the educational and economic development of individuals and communities. In their compilation of recent research on higher education, Pascarella and Terenzini (2005) provide encouraging news about the potential effects of comprehensive community colleges on students' economic and social mobility. Although community college entrants are still less likely to earn a bachelor's degree than similar students who enter a four-year college or university directly after being in school, community college students demonstrate greater gains in their openness to intellectual and racial-ethnic diversity than their four-year college counterparts. Scholars also find (though this has been questioned by Dougherty, 2002) that once students transfer from a community college to a senior college, their chances of

NEW DIRECTIONS FOR COMMUNITY COLLEGES, no. 136, Winter 2006 © 2006 Wiley Periodicals, Inc.
Published online in Wiley InterScience (www.interscience.wiley.com) • DOI: 10.1002/cc.262

graduating are equal to similar students who began at the senior college. Finally, community college transfer students are able to enter more selective senior colleges than they would have originally been eligible to enter. These positive results are most pronounced for low-income students and those with poor records of high school performance.

Open admissions community colleges face a distinct challenge in maintaining quality while managing enrollments. They are unselective institutions that must contend with the popular notion that institutional quality (as measured by admissions selectivity) improves students' occupational status and earnings. Community colleges also face demands from government agencies and accreditation organizations for better retention and graduation rates, as well as postgraduate outcomes, while preserving their commitment to open door admissions (Dougherty and Hong, 2006; Rosenfeld, 1999).

This chapter highlights how Bronx Community College (BCC) in New York employs current business practices as part of an enrollment management program designed to achieve potentially competing goals: maximizing student attainment, preserving open door admissions and a diverse student body, and maintaining fiscal stability. BCC is among a growing number of community colleges using systematic and analytical approaches to effective enrollment management, including Prince George's Community College in Maryland (Clagett, 1995) and the Maricopa County Community College District in Arizona (McIntyre, 1997).

About Enrollment Management

Enrollment management, defined broadly, includes all efforts to manage the size and nature of an institution's enrollment in order to help it meet its goals (Clagett, 1995; Penn, 1999). Enrollment management generally involves developing plans and analyses to shape student enrollment from the initial point of contact with students through graduation (including marketing, admissions, financial aid, and academic advising).

The importance of enrollment management in higher education is widely recognized, yet the focus varies by institutional type. In community colleges, enrollment management helps address institutions' financial dependence on student enrollment, changing demographics, increased competition from other postsecondary institutions, and rising accountability requirements related to student retention, graduation, transfer, and job placement (Dougherty, 2002; Rosenfeld, 1999). Community colleges are challenged to use enrollment management in ways that do not undercut their mission of providing open access to higher education.

Enrollment Management at Bronx Community College

Bronx Community College of the City University of New York has been developing an enrollment management process and system that supports the comprehensive mission of the institution and facilitates student achievement and success. BCC is a good place to study enrollment management processes and outcomes because its student population is among the most academically at risk in the nation, the college culture supports the use of business practices to help students succeed, and tracking transfer results and outcomes is easier at BCC, given the college's position in the City University of New York.

Bronx Community College is a comprehensive community college that serves approximately nine thousand degree-seeking students, with one-half in associate of arts or associate of science transfer programs and one-half in associate of applied science or career-track programs. BCC's students are ethnically diverse (they hail from more than a hundred countries), largely minority (50 percent Hispanic and 43 percent black), and often from low-income families (47 percent report a household income of less than $15,000). Furthermore, most are parents (43 percent are in two-parent households and 36 percent are single parents), many (71 percent) work while in college, and the great majority (88 percent) require remedial or developmental course work (Bronx Community College, 2005).

At a college like BCC, located in the midst of a community that includes many new immigrants aspiring to the American Dream, many students do not have well-formulated, realistic academic and career expectations. This is understandable given that about half of the students are not native-born Americans and the majority are among the first in their families to attend college. More than half the students in the 2005 graduating class changed their major or career focus at least once before graduating (Bronx Community College, 2006).

The BCC enrollment management process is designed to foster the kind of collaborative analysis and assessment that incorporates a number of business best practices, such as *Knowledge Management* and *Business Intelligence*. Knowledge Management, as defined by Bernbom (2000), is "the discovery and capture of knowledge, the filtering and arrangement of this knowledge and the value derived from sharing and using this knowledge throughout the organization" (p. xiv). For example, institutional performance indicators such as course pass rates, retention rates, and graduation rates are generated annually, and along with comparative departmental indicators, are distributed to individual academic and student-support departments to assist them in preparing annual self-assessments and plans. This information provides for contextual and comparative analysis in a relatively nonthreatening manner. Business Intelligence (BI), a term first coined in the 1990s by the Gartner research firm, refers to processes and tools that make information usable to organizations (Quinn, 2003). According to Villano (2005), BI software can deliver specific and targeted information to individual users when they need it, and in useful ways that can lead to effective action.

Bronx Community College has been building capacity to support the use of Business Intelligence and knowledge-based decision making for the past several years. These enrollment management practices are part of a larger effort to embed the use of information and analysis into planning and assessment of all college activities. When President Carolyn G. Williams began her tenure at BCC in 1996, the institutional research and information technology functions on campus were poorly supported and limited in scope. President Williams has promoted a policy of individual and collective responsibility for college activities and outcomes, and broad-based participation in the sharing and analysis of information. More specifically, Bronx Community College has created an infrastructure for information and analysis, built institutional capacity to analyze information, and set expectations for the use of evidence and analysis. Each of these steps is described in greater detail in the following sections.

Create an Infrastructure for Information and Analysis. The college has created an annual planning and assessment program that engages all departments and divisions and encourages the use of evidence for planning purposes and assessment claims. At the outset of each annual reporting process, departments are provided with annual and trend data at the course, discipline, and curriculum levels, which include information about student performance, persistence, completion, and postgraduate performance. Both academic and department heads dialogue with their staff, as well as their vice presidents, in the development of their annual departmental assessment and planning reports. Vice presidents, in turn, dialogue with the president of the college and with each other in the development of their annual division assessments and planning reports, which are used to provide substance to an annual college assessment and plan.

Oversight of the annual and strategic planning and assessment processes is performed by the following entities: a strategic planning and assessment committee (composed of the executive and faculty leadership of the college), an academic committee (composed of department chairpersons), and an administrative council (composed of the administrative department heads of all campus units).

Build Institutional Capacity to Analyze Information. To build the necessary institutional capacity to access, process, and analyze information, BCC made a commitment to substantially increase the number of highly credentialed institutional research (IR) and information technology (IT) staff. Currently, the IR office has three professional staff members, excluding assessment and strategic planning personnel. The college also purchased enterprise reporting software (WEBFOCUS) and invested in the development of a system to convert inaccessible data in a legacy student information system into readily available information in a relational database.

In addition, the college invested in training for senior managers and IT and IR staff in order to build analytical capacity. For example, BCC underwrote the cost of a yearlong training in the use of logic model evaluation methodology for senior managers. The administrative council (which includes all college managers) met every month for a staff development initiative conducted by senior IR staff to learn how to use logic models for identifying problems, developing plans for solutions, and assessing progress and results. Each senior manager developed a logic model project at the beginning of the year, and members discussed progress and helped each other solve analytical and practical problems throughout the year. In addition to building capacity for evidence-based decision making, the process resulted in greater understanding among campus managers about challenges across the campus and effective methods of addressing them.

Subsequent to the training period, the college has also used the logic model format in the development of major institutional grants as well as an updated institutional strategic plan.

Set Expectations for Use of Evidence and Analysis. In addition to the formal planning and assessment structures, the college administration increasingly requires the transparent use of evidence in collegewide decisions. For example, the college senate must rely on data when voting to approve a policy change to the probation and suspension rules, and vice presidents or chairpersons must demonstrate need (based on test scores or course grades) when deciding to offer more course sections. Furthermore, BCC regularly publicizes collegewide assessments and analyses at college events (such as convocations), on the college Web site, and in college publications.

Effects of Using Enrollment Management at Bronx Community College

Two recent examples highlight how BCC used business practices to address the enrollment management challenges of enhancing student success and sustaining institutional fiscal stability. The first example involved a campuswide response to an increased demand for enrollment in the nursing program among students who could not meet the program's entry requirements. In fall 2004, enrollment management team members, nursing faculty, liberal arts faculty, academic advisors, counselors, and research analysts formed an analytical group. Using information from a variety of sources, the group discovered that almost 20 percent of entering freshman students were nursing aspirants. However, only a fraction of that cohort would be able to enroll in or graduate from the clinical nursing program after three years. More specifically, the group reached four findings: the population of nursing aspirants had increased rapidly, few nursing aspirants ever became eligible for the clinical nursing program, demand for the gateway to nursing course (pharmacology) exceeded supply, and overall performance in the gateway course was low. In light of these findings, the analytical group developed several interventions, including creating a systematic application and evaluation process for admission into the gateway nursing course, changing academic policies to limit the number of times students can enroll in the pharmacology course, and providing nursing aspirants unlikely to succeed with advising that would alert them to other academic and career options on campus. As a result of these interventions, the admission

NEW DIRECTIONS FOR COMMUNITY COLLEGES • DOI: 10.1002/cc

processes to BCC prenursing courses and the clinical nursing program are now much smoother. Also, enrolled and newly admitted students have better information about admission into nursing as well as opportunities in other majors. Furthermore, the number of transfer students who are nursing aspirants but ineligible for the clinical program has dropped. The analytical group will continue to monitor and assess these processes and their effects on BCC students.

In a second example, another analytical group (consisting of faculty, enrollment management staff, institutional research analysts, and others) investigated existing probation and suspension rules and proposed a new policy that would better identify students in academic difficulty. Over the course of a year, the group regularly reviewed data (including projections of student performance and persistence based on existing academic profiles and performance) that shed light on the projected effects of various changes to the probation and suspension rules. This analysis prompted the committee on academic standing to propose a policy change to the college's academic senate. The new policy targets academically at-risk students much earlier than before. All students with a grade point average of less than 2.0 (equivalent to a C) are classified as *early warning, probation,* or *suspension,* depending on their credit accumulation and past academic performance. All at-risk students must take some action (such as seeing a counselor, attending a seminar, or reducing their credit load) to address the underlying cause or causes of poor academic performance. As a result of a growing culture of using evidence-based decision making, the college senate now demands evidence of the need for a policy change and details of how it would be implemented.

The positive results of BCC's enrollment management system can be seen in the college's annual performance reports, available on the BCC Web site (http://www.bcc.cuny.edu/InstitutionalResearch/). In addition, as the U.S. Department of Education (2005) has pointed out, "Four-year graduation rates have risen by six percentage points in three years, and nearly five in six students who transfer to the City University remain in baccalaureate education for more than one year" (p. 99). What is particularly important is that these positive results have been accomplished without BCC becoming more selective and restricting its admissions to students more likely to graduate.

Conclusion

The case for increasing the role institutional research plays in enrollment management seems clear. Community colleges will benefit from borrowing business practices relating to Knowledge Management, Business Intelligence, and evaluation practice (which is used in the logic model). Such practices can help colleges serve a diverse and frequently underprepared student population, identify obstacles to student success, and develop solutions to address those obstacles.

NEW DIRECTIONS FOR COMMUNITY COLLEGES • DOI: 10.1002/cc

However, there are many barriers to implementation of enrollment management practices, including lack of infrastructure, time, and knowledge about what constitutes best or even standard practice (Bailey and Alfonso, 2005). Many community colleges do not have the resources to purchase and develop state-of-the art information systems. Indeed, many still rely on legacy systems, where information accessibility is limited. Others are focused on data and information processing but lack the analytical capacity to make sense of the data for effective use.

Clearly, as community colleges build capacity to use business and information tools to manage enrollments and other institutional practices, they need to make sure that their decisions are driven by their missions and ethical principles. Community colleges committed to both open access and high-quality education will be challenged to improve outcomes for their financially and educationally disadvantaged students without undercutting open access. As well, community colleges should avoid using business tools simply as a way of ensuring fiscal stability or accommodating external reporting requirements. Comprehensive community colleges (and those who evaluate them) should continue to judge their effectiveness in great part on the degree to which they provide access and pathways to success to all students. The experience at Bronx Community College is that enrollment management based on the systematic acquisition and analysis of information can improve student performance and persistence, as well as institutional fiscal stability, while still maintaining open access.

References

Bailey, T. R., and Alfonso, M. *Paths to Persistence: An Analysis of Research on Program Effectiveness at Community Colleges.* New York: Columbia University, Teachers College, Community College Research Center, 2005.

Bernbom, G. (ed.). *Information Alchemy: The Art and Science of Knowledge Management.* EDUCAUSE Leadership Strategies. Vol. 3. San Francisco: Jossey-Bass, 2000.

Bronx Community College. *Semester Profile Fall 2005.* New York: Bronx Community College of the City University of New York, 2005. http://www.bcc.cuny.edu/InstitutionalResearch/semester profile.htm. Accessed Oct. 10, 2006.

Bronx Community College. *Enrollment Data Fall 2006.* New York: Bronx Community College of the City University of New York, Office of Institutional Research, Planning and Assessment, 2006.

Clagett, C. "Implementing Successful Enrollment Management: A Conceptual Framework and Two Examples." Paper presented at the 7th annual Summer Institute on Institutional Effectiveness and Student Success, Tacoma, Wash., June 1995.

Dougherty, K. J. "The Evolving Role of the Community College: Policy Issues and Research Questions." In J. C. Smart and W. G. Tierney (eds.), *Higher Education: Handbook of Theory and Research.* Vol. 18. Norwell, Mass.: Kluwer, 2002.

Dougherty, K. J., and Hong, E. "Performance Accountability as Imperfect Panacea: The Community College Experience." In T. R. Bailey and V. S. Morest (eds.), *Defending the Community College Equity Agenda.* Baltimore: Johns Hopkins University Press, 2006.

McIntyre, C. "Performance Based Enrollment Management." Paper presented at the 37th annual Forum of the Association for Institutional Research, Orlando, May 1997.

Pascarella, E. T., and Terenzini, P. T. *How College Affects Students.* Vol. 2. San Francisco: Jossey-Bass, 2005.

Penn, G. "Enrollment Management for the 21st Century: Delivering Institutional Goals, Accountability and Fiscal Responsibility. ERIC Digest." Los Angeles: University of California, Los Angeles ERIC Clearinghouse for Community Colleges, 1999. (ED 432 939)

Quinn, K. *Establishing a Culture of Measurement: A Practical Guide to Business Intelligence.* New York: Information Builders, 2003.

Rosenfeld, S. A. "Linking Measures of Quality and Success at Community Colleges to Individual Goals and Customer Needs." Paper presented at the Independent Advisory Panel Meeting, National Assessment of Vocational Education, Washington, D.C., May 1999.

U.S. Department of Education. *FY04 Performance and Accountability Report.* Washington, D.C.: U.S. Department of Education, 2005.

Villano, M. "SuperData." *Campus Technology,* 2005, *18*(9), 34–41.

NANCY RITZE *is associate dean of the Office of Institutional Research, Planning, and Assessment at Bronx Community College in the Bronx, New York.*

10

This chapter delineates the essential elements of a framework for establishing mission priorities for community colleges.

Prioritizing Community College Missions: A Directional Effort

Christine Johnson McPhail, Irving Pressley McPhail

One of the most contentious and far-reaching issues in community colleges today concerns the institution's multiple missions. Cohen and Brawer (2003) described the community college's missions as student services, career education, developmental education, community education, and the collegiate functions (transfer and liberal arts). We use this definition to guide this chapter's discussions of mission prioritization.

Few would argue that limited funding, the pressure for accountability, changing student demographics, and the public's lack of trust in the higher education enterprise are affecting the operations, programs, and services of the contemporary community college. As these internal and external forces create new challenges and opportunities for higher education, the question of how the community college will respond to these challenges will become increasingly important to the future direction of community colleges (Levine, 2004; McPhail, 2004).

If community colleges continue with their comprehensive mission, they will find themselves competing with numerous other organizations on multiple fronts (Alfred, 1998; Bailey, 2002). Indeed, although those who support multiple missions believe that maintaining them is necessary to fulfill community colleges' statutory mandates, critics believe that community colleges have too many missions and that maintaining all of them makes it difficult to attribute change to one particular mission. This strategy may also deplete resources quickly. As such, the comprehensive

NEW DIRECTIONS FOR COMMUNITY COLLEGES, no. 136, Winter 2006 © 2006 Wiley Periodicals, Inc.
Published online in Wiley InterScience (www.interscience.wiley.com) • DOI: 10.1002/cc.263

mission of the community college may prove inefficient in light of the current trend of diminishing revenues.

We believe that the difficult and critical challenge for community colleges in the twenty-first century will be to determine which of their current and historic missions are viable in today's social, political, and economic milieus. For some time now, we have been concerned that community colleges have been reluctant to prioritize their missions. This reluctance is completely understandable given the historic purpose and values of the community college. However, evidence is lacking to support the notion that all community colleges can sustain multiple missions. We believe that it is time for each community college to prioritize its missions to determine the most suitable for the community served. One college cannot do everything (Bailey and Averianova, 1999). This chapter outlines a framework for prioritizing community college missions.

A Framework for Prioritizing Community College Missions

We suggest a mission prioritization effort now, because we feel that attempting to handcuff all community colleges to multiple missions is unreasonable in light of contemporary economic realities. Our solution is to create a process for prioritizing missions. To do this, community college leaders must revisit their institution's core values to understand what its missions should be. Will the missions remain the same or will they shift? If the missions shift, how can community college leaders prioritize those that are aligned with core institutional values and societal demands?

Prioritizing missions is a more complicated endeavor than it may seem, particularly because there are many perspectives on the definition of the community college's mission. The transfer and vocational or occupational training functions are most commonly discussed in terms of mission. However, when a community college begins the mission-prioritization process, it should take all of the institution's current and historic missions into account.

In addition, when prioritizing missions it is important to consider the year and context in which the college was established; the primary programs and services in each mission; if and how missions have changed to reflect new education movements, address new concerns (such as achievement gaps), and respond to new policies (such as accreditation and state and federal regulations); and if and to what degree each mission is being successfully achieved. Furthermore, community college leaders will need to create an environment where key stakeholders can view the future of the institution and then focus on leading and managing the mission changes that will be required.

In the following pages we introduce an operational framework that can be used to make decisions about mission priorities for community colleges. The six key steps that must be considered in setting mission priorities are depicted in Figure 10.1. We discuss each step in turn.

NEW DIRECTIONS FOR COMMUNITY COLLEGES • DOI: 10.1002/cc

Figure 10.1 Key Steps in Setting Mission Priorities

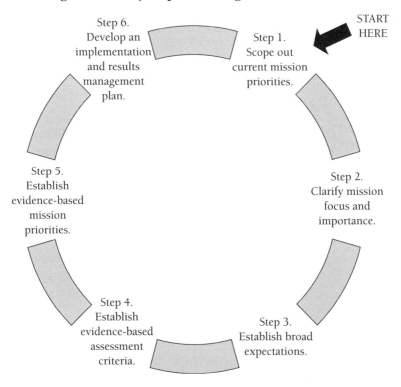

Step 1: Scope Out Current Mission Priorities. The first step in setting suitable mission priorities for the college is the act of *scoping out* existing missions and asking what the future possibilities are for each at that institution. The scoping-out process is depicted in Figure 10.2. As this figure illustrates, decisions about mission priorities result from scoping out the institution's core values, external factors such as changing demographics and business climate, and internal strengths and capabilities. The first step in this process is evaluating the applicability of each mission—student services, career education, developmental education, community education, and collegiate functions—to the college's core values, defined here as the attitudes and beliefs that uniquely pattern the college's organizational culture. As leaders in the learning college movement, we view O'Banion's (1997) six learning college principles as the community college's core values. Essentially, we believe that every mission of the college should lead to improving and expanding student learning.

Thus, the next part of the scoping-out process is determining how each mission affects student learning and skill attainment. Do students know

Figure 10.2. Mission Scoping-Out Process

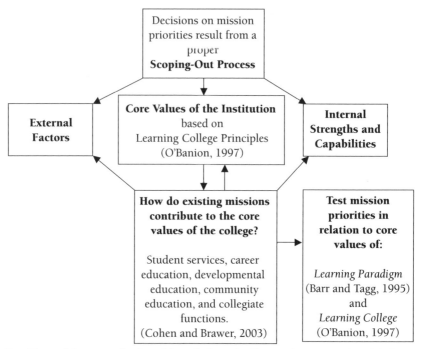

Note: This model was partially adapted from Shirley and Volkwein's (1978, p. 475) model of major inputs to decisions on campus program offerings and priorities.

what you think they should upon completing a program or degree? Do they have the skills necessary to succeed in the workforce or at a four-year institution? The third step is determining the feasibility of each mission, considering quality, need, and cost, as well as current and potential resources available to support the mission.

Finally, a realistic mission priority-setting process must include criteria for measuring the effectiveness and success of the mission. In doing so, community college leaders must keep the institution's core values in mind and prioritize missions in ways that reflect the distinctiveness of the institution and community served. We believe each mission should be evaluated in relation to the core values of the *learning paradigm* (Barr and Tagg, 1995) and the *learning college* (O'Banion, 1997). In other words, how do the programs clustered under each mission improve and expand student learning? How do we know that they do?

Step 2: Clarify the Focus and Importance of Each Mission. After a college has gone through the scoping-out process, several key questions must be addressed before determining how to proceed toward setting mission priorities. We suggest that community colleges ask the following questions: Do all key stakeholders understand the focus of each mission? Are there problems with the missions? Are there opportunities for strengthening them? Are there missions that need to be eliminated or reduced?

Answering the first question requires community college leaders to describe the historic and current features of the missions in their college. In addition, they should describe—in detail—the current and potential value of each mission to the college and its surrounding community. The value of a mission can be described in terms of its usefulness for improving and expanding student learning. It can also be described in terms of its importance as a resource for the college and its local community. In other words, colleges should ask, "Why are we concerned about this mission?"

The next three questions should be addressed in broad terms so that the overall quality of the missions can be assessed. The mission-clarification process should include all internal and external problems associated with a mission. We recommend three filters for clarifying problems and opportunities: quality, need, and cost and available resources. We also believe that the perceptions and feelings of community residents are as important as those of college leaders in the mission-clarification process. All stakeholders, including students, should be consulted in helping clarify problems and opportunities involved in current or potential college missions.

Step 3: Establish Broad Expectations. Before detailed mission priorities can be formulated and specific directions and solutions developed, college leaders must establish the expectations, limitations, and capabilities of the institution. In other words, what would your college like to accomplish? Expectations for mission priorities should be solicited from a variety of stakeholders, including faculty, students, administrators, governing boards, community groups, state agencies (where appropriate), local businesses and industries, and national, state, and local political groups.

In setting mission priorities, it is important to consider the external factors (fiscal resources, changing demographics, state and federal mandates) and internal capabilities and strengths of the college that may affect the long-term achievement and sustainability of a mission. If stakeholders determine that the college can only manage one or two missions, there would be little point in planning to establish five or six. Therefore, mission priorities should be limited to those that are aligned with the institution's core values and can be supported by the institution's existing resources.

Step 4: Establish Evidence-Based Assessment Criteria. An evidence-based assessment of the programs and services in each mission needs to be conducted in order to set mission priorities. The outcomes of these missions, particularly as they relate to student learning, must be assessed to determine which can and should be maintained, enhanced, reduced, or eliminated. We recommend that community colleges assess all basic missions by their quality, need, and cost and available resources. The significance of these categories is that they allow a college to make decisions based on its own data.

New Directions for Community Colleges • DOI: 10.1002/cc

Assessing Quality. Assessing the quality of a mission requires community college leaders to assess the quality of faculty, learning support, technology, facilities, and equipment, as well as student learning outcomes. Clearly, faculty and students are the most important stakeholders in the community college. Therefore, college leaders might ask a variety of questions that deal with important features of mission quality from student and faculty perspectives. For example, what is the level of enrollment in programs under a particular mission? What proportion of the student body in this area is academically prepared? Also, do most faculty in this area teach full- or part-time? How does this situation influence instructional quality? We suggest that the basis of faculty evaluation should be documented student learning outcomes, because if these are low, the institution is clearly not successful in this mission area. Finally, community colleges must examine the quality of student support, technology, facilities, and equipment in their efforts to establish mission priorities.

Assessing Need. To determine need for a particular community college mission, we suggest using Shirley and Volkwein's (1978) idea of centrality to core values, current student demand, and potential demand for programs in a mission cluster. Most community colleges will probably base their needs assessment on what they know about the students enrolled in programs under the mission. A full-scale needs assessment does not need to be an overly expensive or time-consuming exercise. By following a few basic steps, colleges can determine how well pursuing a particular mission currently meets the needs of college constituents and can identify the other types of resources and services the college can provide in the future. A thorough needs assessment can help a college determine how extensively the programs and services offered per a particular mission are being used (and to identify gaps in program and service use); who uses the programs and services, and if there are ways to reach other constituents; how successful particular programs and services are, and how they can be improved to meet the community's needs; whether the college's physical space and buildings are adequate for providing the programs and services per a particular mission; and how student demographics may be changing in ways that will affect demand for the goals of a particular mission. Although no single needs assessment can provide insight into the full complexity of the multiple missions of community colleges, this process will help community colleges prioritize the missions that are most needed by students and the local community.

Assessing Cost and Available Resources. It will be a daunting task to assess cost and available resources, as well as current resource allocation patterns, for each community college mission. Our experiences have taught us that resource allocation sends a direct message about the mission priorities of an institution. Indeed, as go resource allocations, so go the institution's priorities. However, we believe that mission prioritization should be intricately linked to planning and budgeting, available resources, and how those resources are allocated. McPhail (2005) has suggested that although there is no one-size-fits-all approach when it comes to resource allocation, consensus on institutional missions creates a set of shared values and assumptions that, in turn, create a context for program planning, operational planning, and budget decisions. As Massy (1996) maintains, an effective resource allocation process allows a college to achieve an appropriate balance between its identified intrinsic values and those of the marketplace. Institutional resources should be invested primarily in programs aligned with high-quality, high-demand missions that are congruent with a college's values, vision, purposes, and goals, and they should be delivered as productively as possible. For more detailed descriptions about how to rate quality, need, and cost and availability of resources for each mission, see Shirley and Volkwein's (1978) "Establishing Academic Program Priorities."

Step 5: Establish Evidence-Based Mission Priorities. As previously discussed, any effort to prioritize missions entails the difficulties of assessing the effectiveness and accountability of each one. Cameron and Whetten's (1981) notion that we need to understand institutional priorities in the context of effectiveness and efficiency is useful here. They make a clear distinction between effectiveness—or doing the right things—and efficiency—or doing things right. This is all the more important in our current environment of reduced state and local allocations and pressures to hold down tuition and fees. Yet these financial realities mean that community colleges must effectively manage resources to attain and sustain realistic missions.

A mission prioritization plan needs to specify how the effectiveness of various missions will be assessed. This assessment should include an interim assessment of implemented priorities, as well as a plan for long-term assessment. The mission prioritization plan should include a monitoring schedule for each mission to measure its long-term effectiveness in meeting the college's core values, a process to evaluate results and modify mission priorities as appropriate, and a communication plan to inform key stakeholders about accomplishments related to mission prioritization.

Step 6: Develop an Implementation and Results Management Plan. The most important step in establishing mission priorities is integrating the priorities into the culture of the college. An implementation and results management plan must specify how mission priorities will be linked to budgeting and resource allocation decisions. It should include an implementation schedule, a commitment for funding at the appropriate times, a resource plan for long-term operation and maintenance, and an evaluation plan to determine the effects of mission prioritization.

Few community colleges have the capacity or resources to maintain all of Cohen and Brawer's (2003) missions at high levels of quality. Competing programs may reduce each other's effectiveness. Thus, community colleges may find themselves under siege from stakeholders and with few resources to respond effectively. We believe that community college leaders should endorse a business-style approach to monitor the implementation of mission priorities. For example, every mission priority should be defined with clear objectives and measurable returns. Community college leaders should ensure that programs and services under each mission priority include methods to demonstrate quality and data-driven results, and that potential challenges are proactively identified and resolved.

Conclusion

We have offered a model for guiding strategic thinking in resolving critical questions about mission priorities. It is important that community colleges continue to reinvent themselves to buttress strategically agreed-upon visions and directions against external forces that impinge on their work and missions. Mission prioritization will help community colleges fulfill their important promises to students and local communities to provide and promote access, improve student achievement, focus on student learning, embrace accountability, and close achievement gaps between haves and have-nots (McClenney, 2004).

Our framework for establishing mission priorities provides community colleges with a tool to better understand mission priority setting. The framework allows individual community colleges to creatively build on our initial efforts and align mission priorities with the goals and values of their institutions. Some colleges may choose to support one high-quality mission; others may sustain four or five missions, depending on each college's goals, core values, institutional needs, and resources. As community college leaders and others use this approach to prioritize their missions, we hope they will find that community colleges can not only preserve the best of their historic missions but also launch themselves in new and powerful directions for the next generation of community colleges.

References

Alfred, R. L. "Redesigning Community Colleges to Compete for the Future." *Community College Journal of Research and Practice,* 1998, 22(4), 315–334.
Bailey, T. "The Evolving Community College: The Multiple Mission Debate." In N. Thomas, A. Lorenzo, and M. Milliron (eds.), *Perspectives on the Community College.* Phoenix: League for Innovation in the Community College, 2002.
Bailey, T. R., and Averianova, I. E. *Multiple Missions of Community Colleges: Conflicting or Complementary?* (CCRC Brief No. 1). New York: Columbia University, Teachers College, Community College Research Center, 1999.
Barr, R. B., and Tagg, J. "From Reaching to Learning: A New Paradigm for Undergraduate Education." *Change,* 1995, 27(6), 12–25.
Cameron, K. S., and Whetten, D. "Perceptions of Organizational Effectiveness over Organizational Life Cycles." *Administrative Science Quarterly,* 1981, 26, 525–544.
Cohen, A. M., and Brawer, F. B. *The American Community College.* (4th ed.) San Francisco: Jossey-Bass, 2003.
Levine, A. "The Biggest Challenge for Community Colleges: 6 Views. Choosing Among Competing Agendas." *The Chronicle of Higher Education,* 2004, 51(10), B11.
Massy, W. F. *Resource Allocation in Higher Education.* Ann Arbor: University of Michigan Press, 1996.

McClenney, K. M. "Keeping America's Promise: Challenges for Community Colleges." In K. Boswell and C. D. Wilson (eds.), *Keeping America's Promise. A Report on the Future of the Community College.* Denver: Education Commission of the States, 2004.

McPhail, C. J. "The Biggest Challenge for Community Colleges: 6 Views. Staying Focused on Suitable Missions." *Chronicle of Higher Education,* 2004, *51*(10), B11.

McPhail, I. P. "Aligning Strategic Planning, Budgeting, and Resource Allocation in Learning First." In C. J. McPhail (ed.), *Establishing and Sustaining Learning-Centered Community Colleges.* Washington, D.C.: Community College Press, 2005.

O'Banion, T. *A Learning College for the 21st Century.* Washington, D.C.: The Community College Press, 1997.

Shirley, R., and Volkwein, F. "Establishing Academic Program Priorities." *Journal of Higher Education,* 1978, *49*, 472–488.

Christine Johnson McPhail is professor and graduate coordinator of the Community College Leadership Doctoral Program at Morgan State University.

Irving Pressley McPhail is president of the McPhail Group LLC and former chancellor of the Community College of Baltimore County.

INDEX

Back Issue/Subscription Order Form

Copy or detach and send to:
Jossey-Bass, A Wiley Imprint, 989 Market Street, San Francisco CA 94103-1741

Call or fax toll-free: Phone 888-378-2537 6:30AM – 3PM PST; Fax 888-481-2665

Back Issues: Please send me the following issues at $29 each
(Important: please include ISBN number for each issue.)

_____

_____

_____

$ _____   Total for single issues

$ _____   SHIPPING CHARGES: SURFACE   Domestic Canadian

	First Item	$5.00	$6.00
	Each Add'l Item	$3.00	$1.50

For next-day and second-day delivery rates, call the number listed above.

Subscriptions   Please __ start __ renew my subscription to *New Directions for Community Colleges* for the year 2____ at the following rate:

U.S.	__ Individual $80	__ Institutional $195
Canada	__ Individual $80	__ Institutional $235
All Others	__ Individual $104	__ Institutional $269

Online subscriptions are available too!

**For more information about online subscriptions visit
www.interscience.wiley.com**

$ _____   Total single issues and subscriptions (Add appropriate sales tax for your state for single issue orders. No sales tax for U.S. subscriptions. Canadian residents, add GST for subscriptions and single issues.)

__Payment enclosed (U.S. check or money order only)
__VISA __ MC __ AmEx __ # _____Exp. Date _____

Signature _____ Day Phone _____
__ Bill Me (U.S. institutional orders only. Purchase order required.)

Purchase order # _____
                 Federal Tax ID13559302   GST 89102 8052

Name _____

Address _____

_____

Phone _____ E-mail _____

For more information about Jossey-Bass, visit our Web site at www.josseybass.com

NEW DIRECTIONS FOR COMMUNITY COLLEGES
IS NOW AVAILABLE ONLINE AT WILEY INTERSCIENCE

What is Wiley InterScience?

Wiley InterScience is the dynamic online content service from John Wiley &
Sons delivering the full text of over 300 leading scientific, technical, medical,
and professional journals, plus major reference works, the acclaimed *Current
Protocols* laboratory manuals, and even the full text of select Wiley print books
online.

What are some special features of Wiley InterScience?

Wiley InterScience Alerts is a service that delivers table of contents via e-mail
for any journal available on Wiley InterScience as soon as a new issue is
published online.
Early View is Wiley's exclusive service presenting individual articles online as
soon as they are ready, even before the release of the compiled print issue.
These articles are complete, peer-reviewed, and citable.
CrossRef is the innovative multi-publisher reference linking system enabling
readers to move seamlessly from a reference in a journal article to the cited
publication, typically located on a different server and published by a different
publisher.

How can I access Wiley InterScience?

Visit http://www.interscience.wiley.com

Guest Users can browse Wiley InterScience for unrestricted access to journal
Tables of Contents and Article Abstracts, or use the powerful search engine.
Registered Users are provided with a *Personal Home Page* to store and
manage customized alerts, searches, and links to favorite journals and articles.
Additionally, Registered Users can view free Online Sample Issues and preview
selected material from major reference works.
Licensed Customers are entitled to access full-text journal articles in PDF, with
select journals also offering full-text HTML.

How do I become an Authorized User?

Authorized Users are individuals authorized by a paying Customer to have
access to the journals in Wiley InterScience. For example, a university that
subscribes to Wiley journals is considered to be the Customer. Faculty, staff and
students authorized by the university to have access to those journals in Wiley
InterScience are Authorized Users. Users should contact their Library for information on which Wiley journals they have access to in Wiley InterScience.

ASK YOUR INSTITUTION ABOUT WILEY INTERSCIENCE TODAY!

Statement of Ownership, Management, and Circulation

1. Publication Title		2. Publication Number								3. Filing Date
New Directions For Community Colleges		0	1	9	4	_	3	0	8	1	10/1/06

4. Issue Frequency	5. Number of Issues Published Annually	6. Annual Subscription Price
Quarterly	4	$195.00

7. Complete Mailing Address of Known Office of Publication *(Not printer) (Street, city, county, state, and ZIP+4)*	Contact Person: Joe Schuman
Wiley Subscription Services, Inc. at Jossey-Bass, 989 Market Street, San Francisco, CA 94103	Telephone: (415) 782-3232

8. Complete Mailing Address of Headquarters or General Business Office of Publisher *(Not printer)*

Wiley Subscription Services, Inc. 111 River Street, Hoboken, NJ 07030

9. Full Names and Complete Mailing Addresses of Publisher, Editor, and Managing Editor *(Do not leave blank)*

Publisher *(Name and complete mailing address)*

Wiley Subscriptions Services, Inc., A Wiley Company at San Francisco, 989 Market Street, San Francisco, CA 94103-1741

Editor *(Name and complete mailing address)*

Arthur M. Cohen, Eric Clearinghouse for Community Colleges, 3051 Moore Hall, Box 95121, Los Angeles, CA 90095-1521

Managing Editor *(Name and complete mailing address)*

None

10. Owner *(Do not leave blank. If the publication is owned by a corporation, give the name and address of the corporation immediately followed by the names and addresses of all stockholders owning or holding 1 percent or more of the total amount of stock. If not owned by a corporation, give the names and addresses of the individual owners. If owned by a partnership or other unincorporated firm, give its name and address as well as those of each individual owner. If the publication is published by a nonprofit organization, give its name and address.)*

Full Name	Complete Mailing Address
Wiley Subscription Services, Inc.	111 River Street, Hoboken, NJ 07030
(see attached list)	

11. Known Bondholders, Mortgagees, and Other Security Holders Owning or Holding 1 Percent or More of Total Amount of Bonds, Mortgages, or Other Securities. If none, check box ▶ ☑ None

Full Name	Complete Mailing Address
None	None

12. Tax Status *(For completion by nonprofit organizations authorized to mail at nonprofit rates) (Check one)*
The purpose, function, and nonprofit status of this organization and the exempt status for federal income tax purposes:
☐ Has Not Changed During Preceding 12 Months
☐ Has Changed During Preceding 12 Months *(Publisher must submit explanation of change with this statement)*

13. Publication Title New Directions For Community Colleges	14. Issue Date for Circulation Data Below Summer 2006

15. Extent and Nature of Circulation			Average No. Copies Each Issue During Preceding 12 Months	No. Copies of Single Issue Published Nearest to Filing Date
a.	Total Number of Copies *(Net press run)*		1,671	1,673
b. Paid and/or Requested Circulation	(1)	Paid/Requested Outside-County Mail Subscriptions Stated on Form 3541. *(Include advertiser's proof and exchange copies)*	694	674
	(2)	Paid In-County Subscriptions Stated on Form 3541 *(Include advertiser's proof and exchange copies)*	0	0
	(3)	Sales Through Dealers and Carriers, Street Vendors, Counter Sales, and Other Non-USPS Paid Distribution	0	0
	(4)	Other Classes Mailed Through the USPS	0	0
c.	Total Paid and/or Requested Circulation *[Sum of 15b. (1), (2),(3),and (4)]* ▶		694	674
d. Free Distribution by Mail *(Samples, complimentary, and other free)*	(1)	Outside-County as Stated on Form 3541	0	0
	(2)	In-County as Stated on Form 3541	0	0
	(3)	Other Classes Mailed Through the USPS	0	0
e.	Free Distribution Outside the Mail *(Carriers or other means)*		152	145
f.	Total Free Distribution *(Sum of 15d. and 15e.)* ▶		152	145
g.	Total Distribution *(Sum of 15c. and 15f)* ▶		846	819
h.	Copies not Distributed		825	854
i.	Total *(Sum of 15g. and h.)* ▶		1671	1673
j.	Percent Paid and/or Requested Circulation *(15c. divided by 15g. times 100)*		82%	82%

16. Publication of Statement of Ownership
☑ Publication required. Will be printed in the __Winter 2006__ issue of this publication. ☐ Publication not required.

17. Signature and Title of Editor, Publisher, Business Manager, or Owner	Date
Susan E. Lewis, VP & Publisher - Periodicals *(signature)*	10/01/06

I certify that all information furnished on this form is true and complete. I understand that anyone who furnishes false or misleading information on this form or who omits material or information requested on the form may be subject to criminal sanctions (including fines and imprisonment) and/or civil sanctions (including civil penalties).